RESEARCHES

ON THE

TENETS AND DOCTRINES

OF THE

JEYNES AND BOODHISTS

RESEARCHES

ON THE

TENETS AND DOCTRINES

OF THE

JEYNES AND BOODHISTS

CONJECTURED TO BE

THE BRACHMANES OF ANCIENT INDIA

IN WHICH IS INTRODUCED

A DISCUSSION

ON

THE WORSHIP OF THE SERPENT IN VARIOUS COUNTRIES OF THE WORLD

WILLIAM FRANCKLIN

GYAN

Published by

GYAN

Gyan Publishing House
5, Ansari Road
Daryaganj, New Delhi-110002
Phone: 011-47034999, 9811692060
E-mail: books@gyanbooks.com

Distribution Network
gyanbooks.com
India, USA, Canada, UK, Australia

ISBN: 978-93-7169-608-1 (PB)

First Published, 1827

2nd Impression 2025

Printed at: Gyan Press, Delhi.

RESEARCHES ON THE TENETS AND DOCTRINES OF THE JEYNES AND BOODHISTS
Author: WILLIAM FRANCKLIN

RESEARCHES

ON THE

TENETS AND DOCTRINES

OF THE

JEYNES AND BOODHISTS;

CONJECTURED TO BE

THE BRACHMANES OF ANCIENT INDIA.

IN WHICH IS INTRODUCED

A DISCUSSION

ON

THE WORSHIP OF THE SERPENT IN VARIOUS COUNTRIES OF THE WORLD.

BY LIEUT. COL. WILLIAM FRANCKLIN,

IN THE SERVICE OF THE HONOURABLE EAST INDIA COMPANY;

AUTHOR OF "A TOUR TO PERSIA," "THE HISTORY OF SHAH AULUM," AND "AN ESSAY ON THE SITE OF ANCIENT PALIBOTHRA."

WITH PLATES.

"Hæc studia adolescentiam alunt, senectutem oblectant, secundas res ornant, adversis, solatium et perfugium præbent; delectant domi, non impediunt foris, pernoctantur nobiscum, peregrinantur, rusticantur."—CICERO.

LONDON:

PRINTED FOR THE AUTHOR,

AND SOLD BY JOHN RODWELL, NEW BOND STREET.

MDCCCXXVII.

TO

THE KING'S MOST EXCELLENT MAJESTY.

SIRE,

The son of Your august Father's chaplain, the late Reverend Doctor Francklin, after a lapse of thirty-seven years from the commencement of his literary career in the East Indies, during the hours of relaxation from his professional duties, has now the honour to lay at Your Majesty's feet the close of his labours, in the following "Researches into the Tenets and Doctrines of the Jeynes and Boodhists."

The auspicious patronage and protection which Your Majesty has deigned so generously to confer on many of Your faithful subjects, in this bright æra of Augustan literature, impress the Author of the present "Researches" with the hope of obtaining Your Majesty's royal approbation and support; of which, until the end of life, he shall ever entertain the most grateful reminiscence.

SIRE,

Your Majesty's most devoted and dutiful

Humble subject and servant,

WILLIAM FRANCKLIN,

Lieutenant-Colonel, Bengal Establishment.

LONDON, 1827.

PREFACE.

WITH a trembling pen I venture on the widely extended field of Indian mythology; and when I consider the number, respectability, and talent of the eminent men who have preceded me in this line of inquiry, I should be inclined to shrink from the task, were I not upheld by a sense of conscious rectitude of intention, and satisfied that I am actuated by an unabated zeal, however inefficacious it may prove, for the advancement of oriental literature, to which the best part of a chequered life has already been devoted.

A knowledge of the tenets and doctrines of *Jeyne* and *Bood'h* has long in some degree been considered a desideratum among the learned; and though the labours of Wilford, Colebrooke, Buchanan, Mahoney, Dubois, Maurice, and, above all, the enlightened Faber, have contributed to throw a strong light upon this interesting subject, I am hopeful that a few gleanings may still remain to be gathered; and I have accordingly devoted a considerable portion of my leisure hours to the investigation.

Amongst other research, in the pages now offered to the public, will be found a chapter on the worship of the Serpent, and another on the rock-temple and cavern worship exhibited in various parts of the world.

Such are the materials of which the following work is composed; and should the reader be of opinion that I have contributed any additional information to the more recondite researches of my predecessors, I shall think that my time, labour, and expense will not have been bestowed in vain; and I confidently anticipate the generosity of that public which has so often befriended and supported me in the prosecution of my literary pursuits.

W. F.

CONTENTS.

N. B. The Author takes this early opportunity of making an acknowledgement which, through inadvertency, was not placed where it should, more appropriately, have been inserted. From the second line of page 68 to the last of page 72, he has copied, almost *verbatim*, a letter written to him by Robert Wilson, Esquire, M.D. for whose literary favours his obligations are declared in other parts of this volume.

The Author has reason, however, to believe that between this accomplished and ingenious traveller and himself some difference of opinion may exist respecting the application of the matter contained in the passages above quoted.

ERRATUM.—Page 72, line 9, *for* Devanpals, or hordes, *read* Dwarpals, or guards.

ON

THE TENETS AND DOCTRINES

OF THE

JEYNES AND BOODHISTS.

CHAPTER I.

JANNES *, one of the magicians who worked the miracles for Pharaoth king of Egypt, in opposition to those performed by Moses and Aaron by command of the living God, bears, in my opinion, a strong resemblance to the Jeyne or Jain of

* Jannes and Jambros, says Eusebius, were the scribes in religious matters among the Egyptians: they flourished in Egypt at the time when the Jews were driven from thence, and they did not come behind any in the science of *magical secrets*. They were chosen unanimously by all Egypt, and opposed *Museus*,

India; and if we could but trace the colossal figures of this deity to be seen in various parts of the vast peninsula of India, into the land of Egypt or in Ethiopia, the result would be invaluable. It has frequently struck me that these figures may be intended to represent the gigantic posterity of CAIN the accursed; who is mentioned in holy writ as having, after the murder of his brother Abel, the second-born of the sons of men, become an outcast from his family and wandered over the earth with the brand or mark* affixed to his forehead, as a punishment for his crime; and finally, he is stated to have

Moosa, or Moses, a leader of the Jews, and whose prayers were very prevalent with God. Is it not singular that to *this day* the Jeynes and Boodhists are stigmatized by the modern Hindoos as being addicted to magic? On the other hand, Jain or Jayne is derived from Janus of the Romans, who was one of the greater deities, the dii majores, of Rome; and Jayne and Bood'h have long been identified with each other. Janus, when the Latin termination is omitted, becomes Jain; and both Jain and Janus are alike the Transmigrating Great Father, the patriarch Noah, who is the Elder Bood'h of pagan idolatry.—See Collyer's Scripture Miracles, and Faber on Pagan Idolatry.

* Might not the mark or brand which was fixed to the forehead of Cain by Divine command, after the foul murder of his brother Abel, be the prototype and seal of his idolatrous posterity in after-times, and still so visible in the followers of *Siva*, and of *Jeyne*, and *Bood'h*?—THE AUTHOR.

become "the sire of nations," the founder of a race of giants or strong and violent men, who (subsequently) after oppressing the earth, suffered the punishment of their crimes at the general deluge. But their memory and traces of their existence were not ultimately lost, but revived again in the early age of the world after the flood, in a very marked and distinct manner.

The immense size of the Jeyne figures, as described by Dr. Buchanan, in *Canana*, their woolly and frizzled head-dress and their whole costume differing so essentially from those of the *modern* Hindoo deities, all conspire, in my opinion, to induce a belief that they are the representatives of an unique, distinct, and original race, different from all others of the human species, and were doubtless of *Canic* origin.—The learned Maurice, in speaking of ancient worship, has observed that he supposes Casseus, the Cusyapa of Hindoo mythology, is of Cuthite origin, descended from one of the giants recorded in Exodus, as having sprung from an union of the sons of God with the daughters of men; a supposition which their height and bulk appears to justify, and establish them as the *Anakim* or giants of holy writ; and in how remarkable a manner are the Mosaic records confirmed by the whole of the description of this mountain-born gigantic progeny! By Sanchoniatho it is affirmed, that the mothers were of that abandoned class of women who in those days without shame prostituted themselves to any man they met; which shows the increasing depravity of mankind—in exact concordance with the account of Moses, viz. "That all flesh was corrupt before God *."

The learned Wilford †, who has rendered his name immortal by the depth of his erudition in Indian lore, assures us that there exists in India a race of philosophers who spurn the puerile ornaments with which the Brahmin allegories deck their history, and admit *no incarnation of deities;* but insist that the Dewtahs or gods were mere mortals, like the heroes and demigods of Greece and Rome, whom, say they, the Supreme Being was pleased to endow with qualities approaching to his own godlike attributes; and the Hindoos,

* Genesis, chapter 6th.

† See Wilford, Essay, Asiatic Society's Proceedings.

in general, still perform acts of worship to some of their ancient monarchs and sages, who were deified in consequence of their eminent virtues: are not these the Brachmans of ancient India, and the modern Jeynes and Boodhists?

The learned Maurice * entertains no doubt that the elder Bood'h of India is no other than the elder Hermes Trismegistus of Egypt, and that that original character is of antediluvian race; here, then, is an analogy amounting almost to positive and irrefragable conviction; for Bood'h and Jeyne are known throughout Hindoostan, with very little exception, to be one and the same personage. It is the opinion of many learned mythologists who have trod antediluvian ground, that very peculiar and distinguishing marks characterize the *Egyptian Hermes*, viz. to him is attributed the invention of letters, and those innumerable treatises which he is supposed to have written, in theology, astronomy, chemistry, geometry, and other branches of natural philosophy, all which were represented in the solemn processions of the Egyptians, and considered as venerable fragments of ancient

* Maurice's Antiquities, 4to edit.

worship by the hierophant, or chief priest, in the processions in honour of Osiris, or the sun, and Isis: in these, says Maurice, is the patriarch Enoch unquestionably shadowed out, since he is expressly affirmed by Manetho to have flourished before the flood, and to have inscribed in sacred characters the principles of antediluvian astronomy on certain columns erected in the land of *Seriad*, where, we know, for a long time, dwelt the posterity of Ham, under the appellation of *Cuthites*, or descendants of *Chus* *.

Idrees, the Enoch of scripture, is said by a learned Arabian author, called *Albeidawee*, to have been so called on account of the variety of *sciences* in which he was skilled; for the Most High (continues that author) delivered him down from Heaven *thirty volumes:* and he is further affirmed to have been the first callimographist who was versed in astronomy and arithmetic †.

* Bryant's Mythology. May we not hope that many of the undeciphered inscriptions found in Hindoostan may one day serve to elucidate the history of *Egyptian* mythology?—AUTHOR.

† See Maurice's Antiquities.

The Birmans are described by Colonel Symes to be sectaries of Bood'h or Jeyne by Hindoos of all denominations; the former of whom is admitted to be the ninth Outar, or descent of the Divinity in human shape upon earth. Bood'h professed to reform the doctrines contained in the Vedahs, or rather directly prohibited the sacrifice of cattle and the taking away of life in any manner, which the bloody and superstitious rites of the Hindoos admitted of, *even to the shedding of human blood;* as sufficiently appears by the ordinances of the Calica Puran, as described by our countryman Blacquiere *.

For these mild and humane institutions, or rather alterations in the general system, Bood'h is emphatically styled by his followers the *Author of happiness.*

Guadma or Goutama of the Birmans is said to have been a philosopher, who flourished above two thousand years ago: he taught in the Indian schools the religion and doctrines of Bood'h. The image which represents Bood'h is called in the Birman dominions Guadma or Goutama, the Somono-Cuddom of the Jeynes; and this image we find the primary object of

* Asiatic Researches.

worship in all the countries situated between Bengal and China, and extending (as I shall afterwards have occasion to show) to the country of Japan and the Aleutian Isles.

But the sectaries of Bood'h contend, I think with justice, for priority of establishment over the system of modern Brahmanism; and even at the present day hold a balance with them in point of numbers, though the Brahmins possess the spiritual authority.

The Cingalese, or inhabitants of the great island of Ceylon, are Boodhists of the present source, since the inhabitants of Ava or the Birman empire acknowledge to have received their religion from that island. It was brought, say the priests of Ava, first from *Zehoo* or Ceylon to Arracan, and from thence introduced into Ava, and afterwards to China and Japan.

The late Sir William Jones gave his opinion on this subject in direct and positive terms, and expressed his full conviction that Bood'h was unquestionably the *Fo* of China and Japan, and might also be the Woden of the Goths, whose religion, it is well known, once obtained in our beloved Britain.

It may here be noticed, that the *bonzes* of China and the

Rahans of Ava are alike accustomed to wear yellow garments, as being the sacred and sacerdotal colour.

The learned Kæmpfer, speaking of the *Budz** or *Seaka* of Japan, says, "I have strong reasons to believe, both from the affinity of the name, and the very nature of their religion, that its author and founder is the very same person whom the Brahmins call Bood'h, and believe to be the essential spirit of Vishnu in his ninth appearance in the world under this name. The Peguers call him "Samun Khatuma," which is evidently the Somono Cuddum of the Jeynes, and the Cadmus of Greece.

He further remarks, respecting the introduction of Bood'h into China, that about the year of Christ 518, one Dama, or Dhurhum Nauth, a great saint, and twenty-third successor of the holy see *Seaka*, or Bood'h, came over to China from Si-ten-se-ku †, as the Japanese writers call it, (south-east, says Kæmpfer, from that part of the world which lies west from Japan), and at that time laid the foundation of *Boodhaism* in that mighty empire. I shall have occasion to notice

* See Symes's Ava, and Kæmpfer's Japan.

† *Si-ten-se-ku* appears to be the modern Siam.—Author.

this subject when I come upon the progress of Christianity in Asia; a subject which must carry considerable interest along with it in the minds of all who are zealous in propagating the diffusion of our holy religion over the remotest regions of the earth.

Sir William Jones constantly maintained that the Hindoo religion in general has from time immemorial obtained in upper or rather central Asia; and Mr. Panton, in his Illustrations of the Holy Scriptures, describes the striking similarity of manners, habits, and customs observable between the Israelite and Hindoo nations. Abraham is said to be the son of a Hindoo rajah, who, abandoning his caste and native land, which was Mesopotamia, went to reside in a foreign country *.

How far this position be correct, I am not prepared to say; but it is a strong proof of the existence of the Hindoo religion at a very remote period. Nor does it, in my opinion, militate against holy writ, or in any manner tend to shake the foundation of our faith. "† I will make thee," said the

* Panton's Illustrations.

† Genesis, chapter xii. verses 2 and 3.

almighty Creator of the universe to the patriarch Abraham, "a great nation; and in thee shall all the families of the earth be blessed." This gracious promise to Abraham and his seed has been fulfilled to the smallest tittle of verification; nor is there need, on this occasion, to justify a belief in the fact noticed by Mr. Panton *, to ascend to the extravagant and unfathomable antiquity of the modern Brahmins, in their æra of Hindoo mythology.

We are informed that there were two Bood'hs; one of whom is described in the ninth outar, or descent of the deity on earth, as a holy and benevolent personage, who forbade his followers to practise the sanguinary sacrifices of men and beasts on the altars of India. The other, or minor Boodh, is thought by the learned Maurice to be spurious, and to have been melted down by the Chinese into the god *Fo*. This latter, when death approached, is said to have addressed his disciples in the following words †: "Whatsoever I have hitherto told you concerning spiritual affairs

* Panton's Illustrations of the Holy Scriptures.

† Indian Antiquities, quarto edition.

and a future state of existence is nothing more than an ingenious allegory. There are neither rewards nor punishments after life. The principle of all things is an immense vacuum; and human existence terminates in annihilation." Such are affirmed to be the cold, uncongenial, and comfortless doctrines of the younger Bood'h, as detailed by the missionary Du Halde *, which evidently allude to the worship established in China from a very remote period. But the Bood'h of the ninth outar is of a very different description; and, in my opinion, corresponds with the ancient gymnosophists.

It must be observed, however, that though the modern Brahmins acknowledge the elder Bood'h to be the ninth outar, they nevertheless assert that the doctrine ascribed to him is false, and fabricated by some other person. Of this opinion, also, was the late Sir William Jones, who has remarked, that although the most orthodox among the modern Brahmins consider Bood'h as an incarnation of Vishnu, yet they universally oppose the doctrines of the Boodhists with all the malignity of an intolerant spirit; a convincing proof, in

* Du Halde's China, Maurice, and Asiatic Researches.

my humble opinion, that, when the modern Brahmins put down and persecuted the followers of Jeyne and Bood'h, a thousand years since, they determined to inculcate among the followers of their own spurious system * a disbelief and contempt of every thing that before had been held sacred by their adversaries the Boodhists; in order for ever to abolish even the traces of the former worship. Numerous remains, however, of this worship do still exist in every part of India, and more especially in the southern parts of the peninsula, as we learn from Buchanan and the Abbé Dubois. A learned, though unknown writer, who has given to the world much information on the subject of Indian mythology, under the signature of *Manetho* †, has observed, that during a late journey in 1819, he was surprised to meet with the ruins of a mighty temple in the neighbourhood of Mirzapore, an opulent trading town in the zemandary of Benares. He observed, with no small surprise, that this temple had been constructed upon the same plan as that of the *Bora Bood'h*, the great or elder Bood'h in Java; and the amazing multi-

* Manetho, Calcutta Journal. † Ibid.

tude of massy sculptures scattered in all directions proved the richness of the decorations which formerly ornamented its walls *. In a field near this temple appear the ruins of many smaller fabrics, out of which, amongst several fine images of Doorgah, or virtue personified, were dug out two mutilated statues of Bood'h. These statues, says the intelligent Manetho, combined with the other images near this curious spot, prove the religion formerly prevailing in this country to have been precisely the same with that which obtained on the island of Java. He concludes with an energetic remark, of too great importance to be passed over, that the antiquities existing over every portion of this country are not less astonishing than the fact is remarkable, that hitherto they have been in most instances doomed to the most unmerited neglect.

* Calcutta Journal, May, 1819. Article signed Manetho.

CHAPTER II.

ON SERPENT WORSHIP.

"It would (says the learned Bryant) be a noble undertaking, and very edifying in its consequences, if some person of true learning and deep insight into antiquity would go through with the history of the Serpent *." Animated by these words, issuing from the researches of so able a master in the wide field of Asiatic mythology, I shall endeavour, though with unequal paces, to tread in his footsteps.

The worship of the Serpent appears to be of the highest antiquity, and is, no doubt, of antediluvian extraction; from whence, after the flood, it gradually obtained in various countries of the Asiatic world, as I shall hereafter have occasion to show, and ultimately pervaded the greatest part of ancient Europe. In the following discussion it will be necessary, therefore, to proceed in a consecutive series of arrangement and

* Bryant's Analysis, vol. ii. p. 219, 8vo. edit.

order regarding the different countries to be brought under consideration; and as order and method are the proper basis on which a good superstructure can alone be erected, I shall embrace the following details in the order of my narrative:—1. Chaldea; 2. the Holy Scriptures; 3. Egyptian; 4. Persian; 5. Grecian; 6. Roman; 7. Goths and Germans; 8. Hindoos; 9. Mexico and Peru.

In Chaldea * it no doubt originated after the flood, and before the dispersion of the tribes from the plains of Shinar, after the confusion of languages at the building of Babel, or the tower of Belus †, which event occurred by the express ordination

* Chaldea is stated by Maurice to be the original source of the Sabian worship, and the central region in which it flourished; hence the universal and immemorial prevalence of this superstition in every region, viz. the worship of the *Sun* and fire.—In the pyramidal temples of India we see the symbols of the sun's rays darting upwards. In Egypt, in Mexico, and Peru, we perceive the same resemblance; and the Magi of Persia and the Brahmins of India may serve to complete the picture.—Author, and Indian Antiq.

† This famous temple is conjectured by Maurice to be no other than a temple and high altars to the Sun; "erected (as he justly observes) by an idolatrous race who had long deserted the temples and altars of the true God; and it is further stated, according to Herodotus (Clio, 183), that on its vast table or platform, at

of a justly incensed Deity. But we must first ascend to the creation of the world, and commence our inquiries with the grand Serpent of all, the father of lies, Satan the accursed; who was permitted to tempt and finally to overcome the virtue of our first parents, from which source such bitter fruits have flowed into the world, but which in the end is decreed to be rectified; and that decree which went forth against the Serpent after the fall has in all respects and in the most ample manner been completely fulfilled—" And I will put enmity between thee and the woman, and between thy seed and her seed; it shall bruise thy head, and thou shalt bruise his heel *."

the anniversary festival of Belus, the Chaldæans regularly consumed incense to the amount of a thousand talents."—Maurice's Observations on the Ruins of Babylon.

It is singular that the fire *Beltine*, or fire of Belus, and the first day of May, denominated *la Bel-tine*, or the fire of Belus's day, is still preserved in Ireland; that fire is lighted by the peasantry, and that men, women, and children pass through the fire—through flames of burning straw: and it is still more singular that our custom of celebrating May-day by dancing round a maypole should, unknown to ourselves, connect the festival of Belus with that of the Indian *Siva*.—Author.

* Genesis, ch. iii. ver. 15.

In the time of Moses we find this monstrous worship was mixed with the Jewish ordinations, and was in fact practised with the neighbouring idolatrous nations. Among the Israelites in the desert, during their forty years of wandering, as appointed by Divine ordination, we find the Serpent set up in the desert as a sign of consolation to the afflicted, and a pledge of their redemption. This produced a very strong effect on their minds, for this Serpent was in effect a type of our blessed Saviour, and shadowed out his triumph over the great enemy of mankind, in exhibiting the cross stake to which the brazen serpent was affixed, the emblem and prototype of what afterwards took place at Jerusalem; where, as we have seen, the Serpent that had been foretold to bruise the woman's seed was also destined to be trampled on by the victorious Saviour of mankind, in crushing his rebellious head for ever, and obtaining a final triumph over him for the benefit of the human race. The dragon or Great Serpent worshipped in Babylon in the reign of Cyrus, as recorded in the Apocrypha, in the history of Bel and the Dragon, which was ultimately destroyed by the prophet Daniel, affords another instance of the high antiquity of Serpent-worship. By the dragon, says the learned Dr. Gray, is to be understood the great Serpent, the devil, the enemy of mankind, whose triumph was established by that worship, for the time being, and obtained among many nations in early times *.

In every part of the varied and multiplied mythology of the Hindoos one perceives the never-failing emblem of the Serpent; which is always characteristically displayed, either as an ornamental appendage to dress, or as threatening destruction to the beholder, or where symbolizing its prototype when affixed to the images of their gods.

In the Pantheon of the intelligent Major Moor we especially discover these attributes in the person of Mahedeva, the destroying power, as well as in that of Vishnu the preserver, though never in that of Brahma the creating power.

These three personages are well known as composing the

* D'Oyley and Mant's Family Bible; history of Bel and the Dragon, Apocrypha.

Indian *Triad.* In the statues of Bood'h and Jeyne it is a never-failing accompaniment in some shape or other, as I shall hereafter have occasion to show.

Ophiolatria, or Serpent-worship, obtains a station of the highest antiquity in Egypt, and is discernible in most of the ruins of their matchless temples and other buildings for public worship in that wonderful country.

Bryant, in describing the Serpent-worship, observes that the names *Ob*, *Oub*, or Pytho, always imply the prevalence of that custom. He observes, also, that in the orgies of Bacchus the persons who performed that ceremony used to carry serpents in their hands, calling with horrid screams upon Eva! Eva! He however does not admit that Eva meant the mother of mankind as having been deceived by that Great Serpent the devil, or Satan; but rather deduces it from *Epha* or *Opha*, which the Greeks rendered Ὄφις, *Ophis*, designing a serpent; and Clemens of Alexandria has acknowledged that the word *Eva* had properly that signification. Plutarch describes the rites practised by the Thracian women in honour of Bacchus; and Ovid, in the story of Orpheus, has given an interesting and energetic account of the Mænades, or Bacchanalian females of Mount Hæmus *.

In Egypt was the serpent named *Thermutis*, which was looked upon as sacred, and the natives made use of it as an ornament for the head of the goddess Isis, or Parvati of the Hindoos. But, as before observed, the Serpent-worship came originally from Chaldea; and its worshippers, who were numerous, built the city of *Opis* upon the Tigris. From Chaldea the worship passed into Egypt, where, according to Bryant, the serpent deity was called Cneph, Caneph, or Canoph. *Ob* or *Oub* is the same as *Basileus*, the royal Serpent, and named, as before stated, Thermutis †.—But to return more especially to Egypt, from whence this worship passed into Greece, and afterwards to Italy, and finally obtained throughout the great peninsula of Hindoostan, we may notice the prevalency of it in Egypt, the figure of the Serpent being sculptured in most of the temples of the Thebais, where it is a universal orna-

* Bryant's Analysis, and Ovid's Metamorphoses.

† Bryant, passim.

ment, and noticed by all travellers as combined with two other remarkable symbols, viz. the wings and globe; for the wings, the globe, and the serpent form the principal ornament of the temples above noticed. The whole of this mysterious combination may, in my humble opinion, be intended to represent "the Spirit of the *almighty Creator of the universe overshadowing with its paternal wings the terrestrial globe* *." The ingenious and learned Savary, in his Travels in Egypt, has given us an account of the modern Psylli †, or serpent-eaters of that country. He describes them as a frantic race of men, of uncouth aspect, savage, with inflamed eyes and dishevelled hair; as going about the streets of Cairo bearing enormous serpents entwined round their bodies, which they furiously tear and lacerate *with their teeth*, till streams of blood flowing down their bodies give them the appearance of furies ‡.

* The learned Mr. Maurice gives a different interpretation; yet candour will, I trust, admit of two opinions on a subject confessedly intricate.

† Savary's Egypt, vol. i. 8vo edit.

‡ This learned traveller also gives an account of the serpent *Haridee*, which is still worshipped by the priests of Achmoun, though they are Mahommedans.

Is not this a remnant of the ancient *Serpent-worship*, and does it not forcibly recal to our imagination the frenzied oracles of the Delphic priestess in the magical incantations of the Cumæan sibyl?

At, Phœbi nondum patiens, immanis in antro
Bacchatur vates, magnum si pectore possit
Excusisse Deum: tanto magis ille fatigat,
Os rabidum, fera corda domans, fingitque premendo.
Ostia jamque domûs patuêre ingentia centum
Sponte suâ, vatisque ferunt responsa per auras *.

Now through the cave, inspired with rage divine,
She bends with awe to the prophetic shrine.
In vain she labours to *shake off the God*,
To gain the path by mortals seldom trod:
He with devouring flames and raging fires
Pants in her breast, and all her soul inspires;
Till through the *hundred gates*, wide opening, blown,
In heavenly notes the god's response is known.

" This serpent is of the same species with those Herodotus describes, which were held sacred among the ancient Egyptians, who called them agathodaimones (αγαθοδαιμονες), *good genii*; and they were the types of Cneph, a symbolical deity, signifying divine goodness."

* Æneid. lib. vi. ver. 77 et seq.

The Serpent was, moreover, esteemed a type of evil and corruption; and since the deluge, was eminently the fruit and consequence of evil, we find it represented by a serpent, as if it had especially proceeded from the evil principle. Yet was the same animal also deemed a fit type of goodness and wisdom, and as such it was made a hieroglyphic of the Deity; the male serpent shadowing out the great father, or Adam, reappearing in the person of Noah, and the female serpent shadowing out the great mother, or the Ark, venerated in conjunction with the world *. In the Egyptian mythology, the monster Typhon is described as terminating in the volumes of two immense serpents, and is celebrated as the greatest of all the children of the earth. He is said to have overtopped the loftiest mountains; while his two hands extended to the utmost limits of the east and the west. The accuracy of this hieroglyphical painting, which represents Typhon as rising above the highest hills and as spreading himself over the whole globe, will be readily allowed when we find the Egyptians as-

* Faber's Pagan Idolatry, vol. i. p. 440.

suring Plutarch that Typhon was literally nothing more than the Ocean. It is remarkable that the Arabs, who are the immediate neighbours of the Egyptians, still express the general deluge by the term AL TUFAN. The form of Typhon was that of a man-serpent; and the Egyptians, though they allowed him to be the Ocean at the time when the chief hero-god was driven into the ark, evidently considered him also as a type of the evil principle; for, in addition to the sentiments which they entertained of him as the parent of all ill, he is also said to have been the father, by the snake Echidna, of the Serpent which guarded the golden apples of the Hesperides, and which is displayed on the sphere with its head crushed beneath the heel of Hercules*. The Serpent, however, of the sacred garden of the Hesperides was a transcript of the Serpent in Paradise; and we now find it to be immediately connected with Typhon, who was certainly a personification of the deluge, and who was represented under the mixed form of a man and a dragon: consequently, the deluge was sym-

* Faber's Pagan Idolatry, vol. i. p. 440.

bolized, in allusion to the form assumed by the evil principle in Paradise.

It is remarkable that, whenever the Ammonians or Cuthites founded a place of worship, there was generally some legend of a Serpent attached to it. It will be seen hereafter that whenever they migrated, this singular race carried with them their arts and sciences; and they appear, according to the learned Bryant, in various parts of the globe, always great and always learned. At Colchis, at Thebes, and at Delphi this singular worship equally obtained. The Serpent, moreover, according to *Montfaucon*, was a symbol of the *sun*, to which the Egyptians always assigned a place in their temples, and worshipped it accordingly. Eusebius has observed, that the serpent within a circle, touching it at the two opposite extremes of its circumference, signifies the good genius, the *Eudaimon* of the Greeks.

In the 63d chapter of the celebrated Vossius on Pagan Idolatry, a detailed account is given of the origin of the Serpent-worship in various countries of the world. He, with others, affirmed that it commenced in Chaldæa, the place first rendered memorable after the renovation of the world by the family of Noah, and of the earliest postdiluvian records:—"Various causes (says Vossius) are assigned by the ancients for the divine honours paid to the Serpent, since there exists in that animal, exclusively of its advantages of body over all other animals, a spirit of internal excellence which impels it forward in its progress with astonishing velocity, rolling onwards fold within fold in a variety of forms and shapes; and more especially inasmuch as, when it has attained to a great age, after shedding its skin, it is again revivified with efflorescent youth, and appears a fit *emblem* of the divine Providence. It is worthy of remark (he concludes) that God himself commanded Moses to set up the Serpent to the Israelites in the desert *," which, as we have seen, when fixed upon the cross stake, became to them, though they at the time were unconscious of it, an *emblem of the efficacy of the Saviour of the world in the person of our Lord Jesus Christ the righteous.* The beautiful description in Milton will here intrude itself on the ima-

* Vossius de Origine et Progressu Idololatriæ, lib. iv. cap. 63.

gination of the reader, and I may perhaps be excused for offering the passage as it stands in that sublime poem, the pride and ornament of our British tongue.

> " So spake the Enemy of mankind, inclosed
> In serpent, innate bad; and toward Eve
> Address'd his way: not with indented wave,
> Prone on the ground, as since, but on his rear
> Circular base of rising folds, that tower'd
> Fold above fold, a surging maze; his head
> Crested aloft, and carbuncle his eyes;
> With burnish'd neck of verdant gold, erect
> Amidst his circling spires, that on the grass
> Floated redundant. Pleasing was his shape
> And lovely: never since of serpent kind
> Lovelier———————*."

MILTON'S *Paradise Lost*, vol. ii. b. 9, l. 495—505.

* It is a circumstance of a most singular nature, that the great traveller and eminent scholar Wilson has noticed a sculptured representation in stone of Adam and Eve in the garden of Eden, with the serpent rising round the tree. It is to be seen at the ancient temple of *Ipsambul* in Nubia, and is placed in the south-west angle of a chamber in the great cave at that place; and in my opinion most completely corroborates the statement of that event as delivered to us in holy writ.—AUTHOR.

GREECE.

According to Herodotus, almost all the names of the gods of the Greeks were brought from Egypt, from whence they were introduced by Pythagoras into Greece *. One of the principal of these appears to be the introduction of the Serpent-worship from Egypt, which is identified in the characters of *Python* and the Lernæan *hydra* slain by Hercules. This worship afterwards passed into Italy, and is assimilated with the earliest of the Roman divinities. In Greece we have the temple of Apollo at Delphi. The learned Gibbon, our British

* "In the reign of Polycrates, the tyrant or ruler of Samos, the celebrated Pythagoras, one of the most eminent of the Greek philosophers, travelled into Egypt in search of knowledge, and being instructed by the priests of that country, first introduced other kinds of learning into Greece, and particularly a more accurate knowledge of religious rites and ceremonies, of which he was a careful observer—thinking that, although he were entitled to no favour on that account from the gods, he would thereby at least procure esteem amongst men; which actually happened to him on his return, for he so far eclipsed the glory of all other philosophers, that all the young men desired to become his pupils, and all the old were better pleased to see their sons in his company than engaged in the most lucrative and honourable pursuits."—Gillies's History of Greece.

Tacitus, in describing the city of Constantinople *, adverts to the famous *serpentine* pillar situated in the centre of the Hippodrome, called by the modern Turks "*Al Meidan*," or the horse-course. "The circus," says he, "or Hippodrome, was a stately building about 400 paces in length, and 100 in breadth; the space between the two *metæ* or goals was filled with statues and obelisks; and we may still remark a very singular fragment of antiquity—the bodies of *three serpents, twisted into one pillar of brass:* their triple head had once supported the golden tripod which after the defeat of Xerxes was consecrated in the temple of Delphi by the victorious Greeks. The original consecration of this tripod and pillar in the temple of Delphi may be found in Herodotus; and Zosimus, the Pagan historian, agrees likewise with the fathers of the Church that the sacred ornaments of this temple were removed to Constantinople by order of Constantine the Great. Amongst these the serpentine pillar of the Hippodrome and the temple at Delphi were erected in honour of Apollo, in commemoration of his victory over the *serpent Python*."—Gillies, in describing

* Gibbon's Decline and Fall of the Roman Empire.

the site of this famous temple, observes, on the authority of Pausanias, that that branch of the celebrated Mount Parnassus which divides the districts of Phocis and Locris contained towards its southern extremity a *profound* cavern *, the crevices of which emitted a sulphureous vapour that, powerfully affecting the brain, was deemed capable of inspiring those who breathed it with religious frenzy and prophetic enthusiasm. Around the principal mouth of the cavern the city of Delphi arose, in the form of a theatre, upon the winding declivity of Parnassus, whose fantastic tops overshadowed it like a canopy to the north, while two immense rocks rendered it inaccessible to the E. and W., and the rugged Mount Ceiphis defended it on the south. It was over the crevices of that chasm that the *Pythia*, or priestess of Apollo, made her responses, and, inspired with holy fury, uttered those oracles that were afterwards so widely circulated throughout the Pagan world.

Æsculapius, the god of physic amongst the Greeks, has the emblem of a serpent in his attributes, and is in fact identified with *Jeyne*, whose figures are generally described with a ser-

* Gillies's History of Greece.

pent having seven heads enfolded like a turban, forming an overspreading canopy (the emblem of royalty in the East), of which the serpents' heads compose the outer circle, and the pedestal on which they stand or sit (the *Tarat*, or lotus) is embossed round its rim with serpents' heads *. In the Carmen Seculare of Horace † we find Apollo described as the god who is worshipped at Delos, and distinguished by his skill in archery, in allusion to his having slain with his arrows the serpent Python and the progeny of the unhappy Niobe; the former of which actions Macrobius, an eminent naturalist, most singularly and ingeniously interprets to be "*the action of the sun's rays originating intense heat, and producing disease and death upon the human frame.*"

PERSIA.

In the wide regions of the Persian empire we find the

* Can the knobs of woolly hair observable in Boodhaic figures be intended to represent serpents' heads? If so, we have a solution of the snaky heads of Grecian and Roman mythology.

† Hor. Od. Carmen Seculare.

serpent a symbol of the highest antiquity, and holding a conspicuous place in their perverted system of religious worship. In the fire-temples* at Persepolis and Nuksheh Rostum,—for such I conceive them to be,—we observe the superstition of Zoroaster or Zerdusht eminently conspicuous. In one of the compartments of the rock this great lawgiver is described as being encircled with a *serpent*, which serves him as a girdle, and is accompanied by the symbol of the wing and the globe; which mysteriously shadow out the Supreme Creator of the universe; and in Sir John Malcolm's excellent History of Persia we perceive the serpent in one hand of the figure that is said to represent the planet Saturn in the Persian zodiac, as taken from a painting in the *Debistaun*, which is the pro-

* The worship of fire appears to be of the highest antiquity, since we find traces of it in Chaldæa, Syria, Egypt, Persia, Arabia, Greece, and Rome; at which place it obtained in the temple of Vesta (said to be still remaining), and in the offices of the Salii or *priests of fire*, instituted, as I think, by Romulus, the founder of the Roman empire. The Ammonians or descendants of Chus are said by Bryant to have settled on the banks of the Tiber, and brought with them the solar rites, and the worship of fire.—AUTHOR. Bryant's Analysis, vol. i. p. 65, 8vo. edit.

duction of the celebrated Muhussun Fani. In the *Ardivaraf Nameh* *, a work on the religion of the ancient Persians, the supposed place of torment for the damned is "*a dark and bottomless abyss,*" full of scorpions and serpents, which gnaw and sting the feet of the damned: a very manifest and no less singular allusion to the torments of the damned as foretold in Holy Writ.

INDIA.

In the *Courma outar*, or incarnation of Vishnu into the form of a tortoise, to support the earth which was sinking into the ocean, we have the detail of the memorable churning of the ocean (an evident symbol of the deluge), and a particular account of the service afforded on that occasion by the serpent VASUKA. Around the vast mountain Mandar, which served as a churning staff, says the legend, the serpent *Vasuka* was twined in many a fold, by way of a rope, at the head and tail

* This work, published by Mr. Pope of Bombay, is replete with curious information; and the Ardivaraf Nameh appears in all its bearings a complete epitome of Mahomet's celebrated Night Journey to Heaven, as detailed by Sale in his admirable translation of the Koran; and I have no doubt but Mahomet borrowed his Hell and Paradise from the same source.—AUTHOR.

of which those imaginary beings the Soors and Assoors * pulled with all their might, until the fourteen precious gems were produced that had been previously swallowed up by the ocean in a recorded deluge of former times. They now, continues the story, pull forth † the serpent's head repeatedly, and as often let it go, while there issued from his mouth a continued stream of fire, smoke, and wind, which, ascending in thick clouds replete with lightning, it began to rain down upon the heavenly band, who were already fatigued with their labours, whilst a shower of flowers was shaken from the top of the mountain Mandar, which covered the heads of the whole assembly. In the mean time, the roaring of the ocean, whilst thus violently agitated, was like the bellowing of a mighty cloud. Thousands of various productions of the great deep were torn to pieces in the concussion, and every specific being of the ocean, and all the inhabitants of that vast abyss, were annihilated ‡.

* Malcolm's History of Persia. Maurice, Wilford, &c. &c.

† Maurice, passim.

‡ The Grecian story of the Deluge corresponds in a remarkable manner with the Mosaic history. My excellent Father remarked, in his translation of Lucian's

This tremendous description of convulsed nature is evidently allusive to the deluge, and strongly corroborates the opinions of the learned and pious Maurice, who has ever, in his exertions, endeavoured to prove the truth of the Sacred Volume by a comparison with the history and religion of the idolatrous nations of Asia.

The great and many-headed serpent *Ananta*, or *Sees Naga*, king of the serpents, and, according to the Puranas, presiding over the realms below, is stated to have resided in Padalon, or hell, the everlasting abode of wicked spirits. In the fancied representations of the Hindoo mythology, we find the god Vishnoo, or the preserving power, represented as sleeping

Treatise on the Syrian Goddess, that from the Grecian accounts of the general deluge it appears that the present race of men was not the same as that which formerly inhabited the earth, who all perished. The generation now existing all sprang from *Deucalion*, the *Deo-Calyoon* of Hindoo mythology; and that the people who lived before the deluge were proud, haughty, and committed all kinds of wickedness; for which things a heavy judgment came upon them; that the earth on a sudden poured forth great waters, the rains descended, the rivers swelled, and the sea rose to a prodigious height; every thing was covered with water, and all mankind perished. Deucalion alone was reserved to raise up another race, on account of his piety and goodness, &c. &c. See Dr. Francklin's Translation of Lucian, article Syrian Goddess, vol. iv. 8vo. edit. p. 359 et seq.—Author.

upon this enormous snake, whose expanded heads form a canopy for the god, during his repose of a thousand years *.

Sees Naga, also called Ananta, the chief of the serpents, an incarnation of Vishnu in the form of a serpent having a thousand heads, and residing in Padalon, or the lower regions. He is represented as having a gorgeous appearance, a crown set with resplendent gems on each of his heads, one of which is larger and brighter than the rest. His eyes gleaming like flaming torches; his neck, his tongue, and his body are black; his garments red, with yellow skirts, and a sparkling jewel in each of his ears. His four arms are extended, and adorned with rich bracelets: in his hands are the holy shell, the war mace, the chukra, or quoit, and the lotos. The Hindoos likewise imagine that the earth is supported on the heads of Sees Naga, on the horn of a cow, on the back of a tortoise, and on the tusks of a boar.

On an island adjoining to Bombay, emphatically deno-

* The figure here alluded to is to be seen at the rock of Janguira on the Ganges, fourteen miles west of Bhaugulpore.—AUTHOR.

minated the *Elephanta*, from the figure of that animal sculptured in stone near the landing-place, is to be seen the great Hindoo temple dedicated to *Siva*, the destroying power. This remarkable monument of antiquity is too well known, and has been too often described to require repetition *.

It will be sufficient for the present purpose to remark that the principal ornament of the Elephanta temple is a large bust of stone, representing a being with three heads, the middle face of which is presented full, and expressive of a dignified composure; the head and neck covered with ornaments. The face on the left is a profile; the head-dress rich, and the expression of the countenance pleasant. But the head on the right is far different from either. The face is in profile, the forehead projects, the eye stares, and snakes *supply the place of hair*. A human skull is visible on the top of the head; one hand grasps a monstrous cobra de capella, or the hooded snake †, the other a smaller one; and the whole together is about eighteen feet in height, and is calculated, as Mr. Gold-

* See Maurice's Indian Antiquity, vol. i. fourth edition.

† Goldingham on the Elephanta. Asiatic Researches.

ingham observes, to strike terror into the beholders. Here, then, we recognise the attributes of the destroying power in their fullest extent: to which, in many parts on this side of India, is added a cincture of human skulls, completely encircling the body. This remarkable piece of sculpture taken together is intended to personify the three grand attributes, or Hindoo Triad*, in the persons of *Brahma*, *Vishnu*, and *Siva*, for whom Hindoos of all denominations entertain the most profound veneration, and of whom they have formed the most sublime conceptions. An engraved plate of the Hindoo mythology, which I have in my possession, but from whence taken I do not at this time recollect, has the remark-

* The learned and pious Dr. Claudius Buchanan, late Vice-Provost of the College of Fort William in Bengal, in writing to a friend from Bombay, thus expresses himself regarding this celebrated cavern: "I have put them," says he, "on restoring the Elephanta. I found the cavern and figures in a state of progressive annual dilapidation; I have left a memorandum on the subject of improvement and repairing. I have a reason for wishing that the Trinity in Unity at Elephanta may remain while this lower world exists." Pearson's Life of Buchanan, vol. ii. octavo edition, page 169.

These words are remarkable, and would seem to imply that this learned divine had recognised the most essential article of the Christian faith in the sculptured Triad of Hindoo mythology.—AUTHOR.

able figure of a *naked child* standing erect, holding in each hand a double-headed serpent. His right foot rests upon the head of an enormous serpent, apparently in the act of crushing it, and his left on an alligator. The pedestal is a rock. His back is supported by a black stone pillar, and over his head is sculptured a human countenance. The whole is surmounted by a fluted column. In the back ground of the plate are represented figures of animals, birds, and reptiles; among which is the lion, and the stag, and a recumbent sphinx upon a platform; a scorpion, and some hieroglyphics. Of the meaning of this singular plate I am ignorant; but it may probably be intended to represent Bacchus, who is said to have subdued India with an army of monsters, or rather robbers and freebooters, who followed his fortunes from Greece to India. He is described by Horace as *rupibus insidens*, sitting upon the rocks, though here he is in a standing position. He is also represented as *nodo coercens viperino Bistonidum sine fraude crines* *; i. e. binding by force the hair of the Thracian women with harmless serpents, which he carried

* Horace's Odes.

about with him. In this plate, however, we may certainly recognise the attributes of Vishnu, or rather Chrishna. These correspond with the attributes of Bacchus, and Bacchus will agree with the Indian Bood'h *.

CHINA.

It is probable that the Chinese nation are originally derived from that great family of the Cuthites who migrated from the plains of Shinar at an early period after the Deluge, and who also occupied many other regions of the earth. The worship of the Sun and Fire, the religion of these first apostates from the adoration of the living God, has obtained in China from the earliest period; and it is extremely probable that the religion of Bood'h, which now exists in the Chinese empire, was grafted upon that of the solar worship brought originally from Chaldæa by the Cuthites, and afterwards introduced into various regions of the habitable globe. Amongst other traits of Boodhism, the hieroglyphic of the Serpent forms a principal

* Faber, passim.

feature in the mythology of China and Japan, and is there used to express THE DELUGE, received as proceeding from the evil principle; for the emblem of the Serpent partakes both of good and evil. The rout of the great Dragon which had thrown the universe into confusion, according to the opinion of the learned Faber, seems to allude to the same event as the slaying of Typhon, and throwing him into the sea; the submersion of the Titans, or inhabitants of the old world, the casting the serpent Midgard to the bottom of the sea, and the slaying of Python by Apollo after the Deluge*. Before we take leave of Asia, it may not be improper to remark the striking affinity that subsisted betwixt the mythology of Troy and that of Upper Asia, but more especially of Hindoostan.

The learned Colonel Wilford of Benares always conceived the Trojan war, lately the cause of so much discussion in the learned world, to be an imitation of the great war between the gods and giants, or in other words the corrupted state of man-

* It would seem that the great father of mankind, whether designated as Osiris or Dionusus, Cronus or Bood'h, was esteemed in the material system as the "*soul* of the world *(pseukee kosmou)*."—Faber, i. 447.

kind previous to the deluge, which is manifestly shadowed out in that legend. The gods are *Merupa* (Meropes of Homer), and signify in Sanscrit *lords of Mount Meru*, the north pole of the Hindoos, which is a circular spot, and the stronghold of the gods: it is called Ila; or in a derivative form, *Ileyam*, or *Ilium*. There is a Triad (Troiam) of towers dedicated to the three great gods. The Trojans are styled divine, and athanatoi, αθανατοι, immortals; they are Meropes, and came from the place where the *Sun stables his horses*. The gods and giants at each renovation of the world fight for the *Amrit* or beverage of immortality (Nectar), and also for the beautiful *Laeshmi* (or Helen): she is called Helena. In Sanscrit all these derivations,—Meropes, for Merupa, Ileyam or Ilium, Troiam, or Troia (Troja), Helena, or Helene,—are the same, and point to the same thing. The story is told with some variations; and the Trojan war happened soon after the flood of Deucalion, called in Sanscrit *Deva Cala Yavana*, but to be pronounced *Deo Calyun*. Thence a renovation of the world in the circumstance of the great Deluge took place. In a still more rational degree may we observe the traces of Serpent-worship, if we advert to the story of Laocoon and his two sons, as described in the second Æneid of Virgil; who although one of the greatest poets in the world, was no less profoundly skilled in the mythology and history of his own country.

The Trojans, as we find, on the departure of the Grecian fleet for their coast, were preparing to sacrifice to Neptune, when word was brought of the Greeks having left behind them an enormous horse, standing in their now deserted camp.

The detail of Sinon, the Greek, his artful story, the insult offered by Laocoon, in attempting to pierce this enormous image with his spear, are successively given by the poet; but the effusions of his glowing pen, on the termination of this fatal catastrophe, burst forth with a vehemence totally irresistible; and I may perhaps stand excused in offering the description of the death of Laocoon and his two children, in the poet's own words:

> "Ecce autem gemini à Tenedo tranquilla per alta,
> (Horesco referens) immensis orbibus angues

Incumbunt pelago, pariterque ad littora tendunt:
Pectora quorum inter fluctus arrecta, jubæque
Sanguineæ exsuperant undas; pars cetera pontum
Pone legit, sinuatque immensa volumine terga.
Fit sonitus, spumante salo: jamque arva tenebant,
Ardentesque oculos suffecti sanguine, et igni,
Sibila lambebant linguis vibrantibus ora.
Diffugimus visu exsangues: illi agmine certo
Laocoonta petunt; et primum parva duorum
Corpora natorum serpens amplexus uterque
Implicat, et miseros morsu depascitur artus.
Post ipsum auxilio subeuntem ac tela ferentem
Corripiunt, spirisque ligant ingentibus: et jam
Bis medium amplexi, bis collo squamea circum
Terga dati, superant capite et cervicibus altis.
Ille simul manibus tendit divellere nodos,
Perfusus sanie vittas atroque veneno:
Clamores simul horrendos ad sidera tollit;
Quales mugitus, fugit cum saucius aram
Taurus, et incertam excussit cervice securim.
At gemini lapsu delubra ad summa dracones
Effugiunt, sævæque petunt Tritonidis arcem:
Sub pedibusque Deæ, clypeique sub orbe teguntur *."

It is singular that in the time of Pausanias we find a statue

* Virgil, second Æneid.

of the goddess Minerva was to be seen at Argos, sculptured out of the finest Parian marble, in which two serpents are represented as enfolded at the feet of the goddess, and protected by her shield; a memorial, as it would appear, of the circumstance above recorded.

SOUTH AMERICA.

If the worship of the Serpent, as we have seen, obtained so universally over the old world, it is no less certain that we find it in the new; for not only was the Serpent venerated as the greatest of gods by the Russians and other northern nations, but it found its way, by what channel is uncertain, into South America, and formed a principal feature in the worship of Mexico and Peru *. The god *Vitzliputuli*, the Mexican deity, was carried from one place to another in an ark, like

* It would be a question of curious import to ask, whether the old world had connexion with the new *by land* previous to the discovery of Columbus, and by *what channel?* for how else can we account for the similarity of worship obtaining in both? If by land, they must have crossed over by the N.W. coast of America, and through those regions of thick-ribbed ice which have baffled the successive efforts of modern navigators.—AUTHOR.

Osiris or Dionusus. He was, according to Faber, the great Father of Mexican mythology; and held in his right hand a staff cut in the form of a serpent, whilst the four corners of the ark terminated in carved representations of serpents' heads —a manifest symbol of eternity.

In Mexico more especially, we find the celebrated Serpent Woman, termed by the Mexicans *Cihnacohnatziti*, or *woman of our flesh*, i. e. the great Mother of mankind. She is the companion of Tonacatrewtra, or the great Father; and she is universally represented with a great Serpent.

In fact the father and mother of mankind in all idolatrous countries have ever been symbolized by the great male and female Serpent, and consequently the object of veneration by their misguided followers *.

SCANDINAVIA OR GOTHLAND (RUNIC).

Quitting the eastern hemisphere, we must now direct our course westward, and, after traversing the wilds of Siberia and

* Humboldt's Researches, translated by Miss Williams, vol. i. 8vo edit.

the vast extent of the Russian empire, approach the confines of Scandinavia and the extreme point of Northern Europe; whence, after tracing the outlines of Runic mythology, we shall pass over to the druidical rites of the Isle of Anglesea, the Mona of the Romans, on the shores of our beloved Britain.

The evil Being of the GOTHS is said to have had two children, Death, and an immense Serpent. The universal Father (says the Edda of the Goths) despatched certain of the gods to bring these children to him: when they were come, he threw the Serpent down to the bottom of the ocean, but there the monster waxed so large that *he wound himself around the whole globe of the earth* *. "The Serpent," says the learned

* Lord Byron, in his "*Cain*, a Mystery," has spiritedly described the Serpent which Cain saw in Hades. It bears a strong resemblance to that of Midgard, above noticed.—The AUTHOR.

> "———————— Yon immense
> Serpent, which rears his dripping mane and vasty
> Head ten times higher than the haughtiest cedar,
> Forth from the abyss looking as he could coil
> Himself around the orbs we lately looked on:

Faber, "is cast down to the bottom of the ocean, but he soon encompasses the whole earth in his enormous folds*.—Language," continues this acute and able observer, "cannot better describe the fate of the *apostate* Angel and his universal dominion over man in his natural state, than this *emblematical* and truly terrific account." Further he observes, whilst treating on the Gothic or Runic mythology, that THOR is represented as the first-born of the supreme God, and is styled in the Edda "the eldest of sons†." He was esteemed in Scandinavia as a middle divinity, a *mediator* between God and man. He is moreover especially said to have bruised or beat to pieces the head of the great Serpent *Midgard* with his battle-axe‡, to have felled

Is he not of the kind which basked beneath
The tree in Eden?"

Lord BYRON's *Cain*, p. 395.

* Faber's Horæ Mosaicæ, vol. i.

† Faber, ibid.

‡ It is curious that the battle-axe of Thor the Runic deity, which is cruciform, and is termed by the Scandinavians the *hammer*, should resemble an emblem of the worship of Jeyne and Bood'h, as described in the Pantheon of Major Moore; and is noticed by the ingenious Mr. Hobhouse in his Illustrations of Lord Byron's Childe Harold, where the *Hammer of Thor* is given in the following forms:—

him to the earth; but not until the deadly venom that flowed from the Serpent's mouth had stifled the victorious monarch with its pestiferous exhalations: and he fell back nine paces (says the account) and expired. Here then from a Pagan source we have in a remarkable manner a confirmation of the promise made in holy writ, viz. that "the seed of the woman should bruise the Serpent's head," but that "the Serpent should bruise his heel *." It is to be observed that the Gothic nations were originally a branch of the Chusas or Cuthites, descendants of Chus, who emigrated into Europe from their ancient settlements in the Indian Caucasus, and brought with them into the West the mythology of their brethren of Hindoostan, who are termed by Bryant Indo-Scythians. In fact the great Serpent Midgard, before noticed, is nothing more than a representation of the Egyptian fable of Typhon,

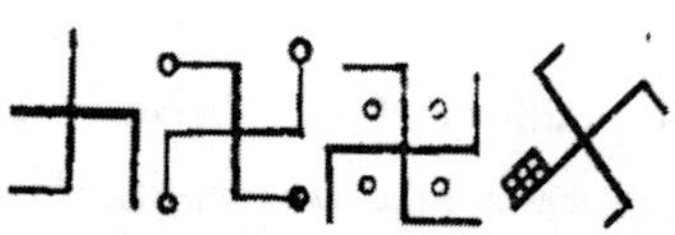

The coincidence is striking and singular.—See Moore's Pantheon, and Hobhouse's Illustrations of Childe Harold, p. 341, 8vo. edit.

* Genesis.

in which the general prevalence of the deluge is shadowed out. Thor is melted into Woden, who is in fact the Bood'h of India, and is the great Father, who is affirmed, in the mythology of Scandinavia, to have embarked in the boat to fish for the Serpent Midgard, and to have dragged him by force from his watery bed *.

* Thor (says the Edda) told the giant Eymer that they had better go a good way further; accordingly, they continued to row on, till at length Eymer told him, that if they did not stop they would be in danger of the Great Serpent Midgard. Notwithstanding this, Thor persisted in rowing further; and, spite of the giant, was a great while before he would lay down his oars. Then, taking out a fishing-line, extremely strong, he fixed to it the ox's head, unwound it, and cast it into the sea. The bait reached the bottom; the serpent greedily devoured the head, and the hook stuck fast in his palate. Immediately the pain made him move with such violence, that Thor was obliged to hold fast with both his hands by the pegs which bare against the oars; but the strong effort he was obliged to make with his whole body caused his feet to force their way through the boat, and they went down to the bottom of the sea, whilst with his hands he violently drew up the serpent to the side of the vessel. It is impossible to express the dreadful looks that the god darted at the serpent, whilst the monster, raising his head, spouted out venom upon him. In the mean time the giant Eymer, seeing with affright the water enter his bark on all sides, cut with his knife the string of the fishing-line, just as Thor was going to strike the serpent with his mace. Upon this the monster fell down again to the bottom of the sea: nevertheless

GREAT BRITAIN.

The Isle of Anglesea *, at the western extremity of North Wales, is supposed to be the most ancient seat of the druids in Britain. Geographers have stated it to be 24 miles in length by 14 in breadth. It is separated from Carnarvonshire by a long and narrow strait called the Menai, from whence the Romans gave the island the appellation of *Mona*. That part of the island adjoining the strait is still finely wooded, and recals to the mind of the antiquary its ancient situation when the druidical rites were performed amid the gloom of its thickest groves †. Rude mounds of earth and heaps of

(some add that) Thor darted his mace after him, and bruised his head in the midst of the waves."—See Mallet's Northern Antiquities, in 2 vols. Edinburgh, 1809.

* Who can name the Isle of Anglesea, and not associate with it that of the gallant Marquis who fought with Wellington in the field of Waterloo? A *brother Westminster* willingly pays this tribute, so justly due to valour and merit.—Author.

† "Druidism," says the learned Davies, "as we find it in British documents, was a system of superstition composed of heterogeneous principles. It acknowledges certain divinities, under a great variety of names and attributes. These

massive stones are still to be seen in this island, indicating the remains of druidical temples. Within this line of woods which fringe the Strait of Menai the country appears naked, though watered by many streams, and affording an abundant supply of grass and corn for the numerous herds of cattle which occupy this part of the island, many thousand head of which are annually transported over the Ferry of the Menai

divinities were nothing more than deified mortals and material objects *mostly connected with the history of the Deluge*; but, in the progress of error, they were regarded as symbolized by the sun, moon, and certain stars, which in consequence of this confusion were venerated with divine honours. The superstition apparently arose from the gradual or accidental corruption of the patriarchal religion, of the abuse of certain commemorative honours which were paid to the ancestors of the human race, and by the admixture of the *Sabian* mythology." This in a remarkable degree illustrates the system of Pagan idolatry throughout the world, as not only in India and China were the favourite deities chosen from deified mortals, but the systems of Egypt, Greece, and Rome, are evidently to be traced as springing from similar sources.

It would appear, then, that the line of connexion with regard to Pagan mythology and idolatry will run thus: viz. Chaldæa, Egypt, Greece, Rome, Germany, Gaul and Britain; from Egypt into India, Tibet, Bootan, Tartary, to Ava, Siam, Ceylon, and to the isles of the Eastern Archipelago, Japan and China, and from thence to Siberia, Russia, Scandinavia, and the northern extremities of Europe.—AUTHOR.

to the mainland. In the Isle of Anglesea is a mountain called *Parys* *, or Parus, famous for its copper mine; and to the N.W. is a quarry of green marble intermixed with the substance called asbestos: such are the productions of this singular isle. The similarity of the laws and customs of the Druids and ancient Brahmins has been remarked by a variety of writers, and it is beyond doubt that the hierarchy of the Druids was a ramification of the worship of the Hindoos: their offices and privileges were of a similar nature, they administered all the religious ceremonies, they managed the sacrifices, and instructed the people, by whom to the present day, among the Hindoos, they were considered as the oracles and depositaries of every thing learned and instructive which belonged to the times; above all, *Abaris* or *Bladud*, the high-priest of the Druids, who is said to have instructed Pythagoras the Samian philosopher, was in fact no other than the *Puttee Gooroo* † of Hindoostan, and the Archimagus or Peer-i Moghaun of the Persians.

* Can the derivation of this name bear any analogy to the *Parus Nauth* mountain in Hindoostan, the chief seat of the Jeyne worship at the present day?

† *Puttee Gooroo*, "lord of priests," Hindu.

The transmigration of the soul, the metempsychosis of the Greeks, was amongst the Druids a leading principle: they worshipped various divinities, and sometimes offered human sacrifices to senseless idols.

Among the rites of Druidism, it was the human sacrifice which chiefly astonished and excited the abhorrence of the nations of Europe. But this sanguinary immolation, it would seem, was by many understood to be a mystical sacrifice, and a typical representation of the great vicarial sacrifice that was to come. For it was after the Phœnician colonies had mixed with the primæval Britons, that the degenerate priesthood of the Druids delighted in human blood; and their victims, though sometimes beasts, were oftener men; since a leading principle of Druidism was, "pro vitâ hominis nisi vita hominis redditur, non posse aliter deorum immortalium numen placari." The life of a man must be the sacrifice for all men, and without this the favour of the immortal gods was not to be expected: a singular doctrine, but practised in several parts of the ancient world *.

* Polwhele's History of Devonshire, folio, vol. i. page 141. Druids.

The funeral rites of the Druids also partook strongly of the eastern character. They burnt the body on the pile, and often the favourite wife or slave. From hence it may fairly be inferred that the Druids were descended from an Asiatic stock; and the physical character of this people will, it is affirmed, bear out the foregoing proposition.

The Druids were dark in their complexion, with high cheek-bones, and the head partaking of the Tartar outline; characteristics which are still observable amongst their supposed descendants, the Highlanders and the Welsh *.

The stupendous ruins at Stonehenge in Wiltshire are doubtless the remains of a druidical temple. They lie on Salisbury plain, about six miles north of the city. This temple was of a circular form, and dedicated to the great solar orb, as is evident from its *serpentine* form; that animal, as we know, being always considered as an emblem of the great father of light †. It is of a circular shape, or rather circle within

* Calcutta Journal, 1821.

† In John Wood's account of Stonehenge, we find the following remarkable solution of the causes which originated the fashion of that remarkable edifice, which I shall give in the words of this ingenious architect and learned antiquary.

circle, like the folds of the serpent. This magnificent temple * was denominated by the ancient Britons the Mundane Circle of Stones, the Circle of the World, or the mound constructed of stone work, representing the circle of the world †. Each of the Trilithons, or triplestones, as they are called by Stukeley, formed a noble portal; and through these portals (which primarily represented the door of the Ark, but were afterwards considered astronomically as the doors of the sun, the moon,

"Now," says Mr. Wood, "if we turn to our antiquity, the two outward rows of pillars are the very emblems of the two first principles of the Magian religion; for the colour of the stones intimate good and evil; and the lines which these stones form, being the peripheries of circles, or lines returning into themselves, represent eternity.

But the two inward rows of pillars vary the principles pointed out by the former; for notwithstanding the colour of the stones intimate good and evil, yet the imperfection in the lines which these stones form, as they are partly curved and partly straight, without returning into themselves, denotes created things, and exhibits the reformation which Zoroaster made in the Persian theology, by divesting the two first principles of it of eternity, and making light and darkness works of the supreme God." Wood's Stonehenge Explained, London, 1747. Letter to Lord Oxford, 8vo edit. page 92.

* Davies's Mythology of the British Druids; and Faber, passim.

† Stukeley's History of Stonehenge.

and the planets), the aspirant, or person to be initiated into the mysteries of the solar rites, was conducted into the interior, and was supposed to become regenerate by the efficacy of this holy operation. The edifice was composed of two concentric circles, enclosing an elliptical adytum, or cell; and in the centre was a large flat stone, placed there as an altar *. In this temple the god *Hu* was venerated as the serpent god; and to that circumstance may be ascribed the serpentine figure attached to the ring of Abury †. The two together formed the hieroglyphic of the serpent; and as the serpent god is always represented with wings, the whole composed the

* J. Wood, the eminent architect, in his account of "Stonehenge Explained," says, that the whole edifice may be looked upon as an emblematical epitome of the greatest part of what our ancient priests of the oak held to be sacred, and in which they instructed their pupils. It was in fact the *Ambert Khend* of the British Druids, which, like the *Ambert Khend*, or probably *Amrit Khoond* of the Indian Hylobii, contained all their sacred doctrines.—*Wood's Stonehenge Restored*, Oxford, 1747, 8vo edit. page 83. The Hylobii of ancient India were doubtless the author's Brachmanes of Arrian and others; consequently the ancestors of the modern Jeynes and Boodhists.—AUTHOR.

† Abury. The circle at Abury enclosed two other circles, and was attached to an enormous snake, formed entirely of upright stones, with a fourth circle for its head. Faber, ibid.

famous Egyptian hieroglyphic so frequently noticed in the course of this discussion, namely, the wing, the globe, and the serpent. It is to be remarked, from the same authority, that the god *Hu* above noticed, or, as sometimes termed, *Noe*, (which is very significant), as the allegorical husband of the ship-goddess *Ceridwer** (who is described as having been preserved in the ark at the universal Deluge) is styled in the writings of the ancient British bards "the glancing *Hu*, the gliding king, the dragon sovereign of Britain †." If, as has been frequently supposed, Bood'h was the type of the sun, the great solar orb, we may reasonably conclude that the magnificent temple of Stonehenge was dedicated to Bood'h. Bood'h, according to Bryant, is the sun: Shems or Shemes, شمس بيت السمس (Beit Shemesh), "the sun's house." He is also Sam, Sham, Samen, Samanean, Somonaouddum, or Cadmus of the Greeks, and finally Somona ‡ Bood'h, the god of the

* The British Ceres.

† Faber's Pagan Idolatry.

‡ *Somona* or Samana, in the language of Thibet and Bootan, implies "the holy one."

sect called Samana Boodhists, discernible in various parts of India. Let Dionuses, or Bacchus, or Bood'h be diversified ever so much, and by ever so many names, says the learned Bryant, they all, in respect to worship, relate ultimately to the sun *. It would appear, then, that the royal sacred Serpent of Egypt, the Serpent Canuphis or Cneph, as seen in the temples of the Thebais; the serpentine deity of Persia, as represented on the walls of Persepolis, and at Nukshi Rustan; the serpentine devices of the Chinese; the globe and winged Serpent of the Chaldean magi; the great Serpent Ananta, Sees Naga, and Vasuka of Hindoo mythology; the Mexican Serpent, and the Midgard of Scandinavia,—all spring from one and the same source, and all bear the same relative meaning, viz. *symbolically shadowing out the power and wisdom of the*

The idols of the ancient Britons and Saxons were as follows: —1. The sun; from whence our *Sun*day. 2. The Moon; *Mon*day. 3. Tuisco; *Tues*day. 4. Woden, Odin, and Bood'h; *Wednes*day. 5. Thor; *Thurs*day. 6. Freiga; *Fri*day. 7. Seater, or *Satur*day (probably *Saturn*), composing the seven days of our British week.—AUTHOR.

* "Sit Osiris, sit Anuphis, Nilus, Siris, sive quodcunque aliud ab Hierophantis usurpatum nomen, ad unum tandem SOLEM, antiquissimum gentium numen, redeant omnia."—Selden, apud Bryant.

Supreme Creator of the universe to all eternity: a striking coincidence, and in a very remarkable degree illustrative of the general principles of Pagan superstition *.

* See Bryant's Mythology, Chardin, Le Brugne, Kæmpfer, and Maurice.—Quere, Will not Cneph of the Egyptians answer to the Arabic نفس Nefus, soul or spirit?—AUTHOR.

CHAPTER III.

ON THE CAVERN AND ROCK TEMPLES, COLOSSAL FIGURES, AND HIGH MOUNTAINS OF THE JEYNES AND BOODHISTS, IN VARIOUS PARTS OF ASIA AND AFRICA.

THE great works of antiquity observable in various parts of Asia, but particularly in the widely extended peninsula of Hindoostan, are undoubtedly of CUTHIC origin; *i. e.* according to the learned Bryant *, of Indo-Cuthites, who came into India at a very early period after quitting their native country of Ethiopia. Here they came under the appellation of *Indi*, *Sindi*, Arabes, and Ethiopians †; and it should seem that not only the magnificent temples of Ellora in the Dekhan were the work of this ingenious race, but that in various other parts of the world works of equal magnificence were erected

* Bryant's Analysis, vol. v. 8vo.

† Bryant, passim.

by them; that they were the builders of the great temple of Belus, or the sun, in Chaldea, of the mighty Babylon; in after-times, of *Baal Bek* in Syria, of the pyramids of Egypt, and the stupendous palace of Persepolis or Istuckar. But we must confine ourselves for the present to Hindoostan.

Salsette, near the island of Bombay, is divided from that island by a narrow arm of the sea. In the centre of Salsette are the celebrated excavations or caverned chambers of Canara *. They are embosomed in extensive woods, and present a view of four distinct hills, which appear at a distance to be one entire rock. On the sides are the caverns hewn out of the living rock, the work of an age too remote to be traced,

* Maurice, Faber.

It is the general belief among the Eastern nations, that the more noble buildings of the antediluvian world were not destroyed; and many temples are still extant that have been originally excavated from the solid rock, which could not be injured by time, climate, or the flood of the Deluge, and were most unquestionably the works of the artists of the old world. Such I conceive to be the splendid ruins at the caves of Canara and Salsette, the excavated temples at Ellora in Dekhan, the grottoes at Thebes in Upper Egypt, and the excavated chambers at Persepolis.

but no doubt of Cuthic origin. Long galleries without lead to the separate ranges of apartments in the interior, and in the recesses of those is displayed aloft in a *conical form*—the celebrated Phallus, the impure emblem of the worship of Siva.

The western hill contains the chief temple of the island, which has an arched, instead of a flat roof like the others, and in its conformation bears a strong resemblance to a natural grotto—*nympharum domus.*

This temple is eighty-four feet in length, forty-six in breadth, and forty feet in height. In the vestibule are two colossal statues, probably Jeyne, each twenty-seven feet high, and are stationed like porters or door-keepers, to guard the entrance of the temple. In these we recognise the Byroo, or door-keeper of Mahadeo in Upper Hindoostan. Thirty-five massy pillars support the roof, and at the extremity is the usual colossal conical stone, twenty-seven feet high and twenty in diameter.

Above these excavations the rocky ascent rises pyramidically in four peaks, and the summit is gained by an ascent of steps cut out of the solid rock. The top, like the pyramids of Egypt, was most probably used for the double purpose of sacrifice and astronomical observations*, in order to typify the father of mankind as the humble worshipper of the great and living God.

From Salsette bending our steps to the south-east, in the Dekhan, we arrive at the caves of Ellora, eighteen miles distant from the city of Arungabad. They consist of numerous excavations in a rocky mountain, forming a semicircle of two hundred yards. The largest of the caves is called *Cailasa*, or paradise, and many paradises are to be found in Hindoostan.

A beautiful stone temple is formed out of the solid rock, and adorned, both inside and without, with a variety of figures in bas-relief. Between the scarp of the rock and the temple is a spacious veranda or portico, under which are to be seen fifty gigantic figures, the colossal representatives of Jeyne and Bood'h. The dimensions of this cavern are two

* Maurice's Indian Antiquities.

hundred and forty feet in length by a hundred and forty in breadth, and the scarp of the rock ninety feet in height. These stupendous caverns are doubtless of Cuthic origin *.

The Cuthites †, or descendants of Chus, after being broken

* There are many statues also of the modern system of mythology intermixed with the colossal Jeynes above mentioned. This has puzzled many learned persons to account for the apparent jumble of divinities; but, in my humble opinion, it may be easily solved if we suppose that the modern statues have been restored by the Hindoos, subsequent to the persecutions of the Jeynes and Boodhists about one thousand years back.—AUTHOR.

† A very important remark respecting these Cuthites is given by the learned Bryant, who, in tracing the wide extent of their migrations and journeys, has observed with respect to the Chaldeans, that Ham, Chus, and Nimrod, the three Noachidæ, were the heads of this nation; and that the Chaldeans being the most ancient inhabitants of that country, there are no other heads of families to whom we can properly refer their origin: they were, according to this author, the most early constituted of any people upon earth, and, from their situation, it is evident that Chus was the head of the family, and Nimrod the first who bore royal sway. They seem to be the only people who did not migrate immediately after the general deluge, and the centre of their abode was at Ur in Chaldea, not far from the conflux of the Euphrates and Tigris, the modern Coorna, in the vicinity of Bussora, at the head of the Arabian Gulf.

From hence, in after time, they gradually extended themselves under the names of Cusaans, or Cuthites, as far as Egypt west and the Ganges east, occupying to and dispersed from Shinar, the just punishment for their impious attempt to erect the Tower of Babel, wandered, in detached masses, to many different regions of the earth. They subdued many countries, and wherever they went they carried their own superstition along with them, viz. the worship of the sun and fire, totally different from the pure patriarchal worship of their great progenitor the pious Noah. Hence, according to Bryant, Faber, and others, arose the striking resemblance between the religious system of so many different countries, all of which had been either conquered or visited by the Cuthites, and all had imbibed the same species

the south all the Asiatic sea-coasts and the whole of the continent of Arabia. In process of time they obtained possession of the coasts of Africa upon the Mediterranean, and even to the Atlantic, and advanced as far as Fez and Tafilet, the present empire of Morocco. In these countries they afterwards consolidated their authority, and during the early conquests of the Mahometans, under the appellation of Saracens, or Traversers of the Desert, Sehara Zun, striking the desert, صحرازن established that mighty empire, which was swayed by the Caliphs from Bagdad to Tibet, and from the pillars of Hercules to the extremity of the Nubian desert and the confines of Hindoostan. Bryant's Analysis, and Ockley's History of the Saracens.

of idolatrous superstition, from the uttermost parts of Asia and Africa to the extreme shores of Europe.

The caves of Salsette and Elephanta doubtless were known to the Greeks, and the same sort of worship existed at the time of Alexander's invasion as at the present moment; for, in the fifth book and the third chapter of Diodorus Siculus, we have some remarkable observations regarding the holy islands, and Panchæa of the Greeks. These islands are said to be on the confines of the Indian ocean, and the inhabitants worshippers of Jupiter Triphylius, in a temple of white marble two hundred yards in length, and as many in breadth, supported by thick pillars, curiously adorned with carved work, in which are placed huge statues of the gods. The priests have apartments around the temple, and in them is vested the sole power of the state; they are the only arbitrators in controversial points, both civil and religious, and are also the receivers of the revenue; they have fine garments of sheep's wool, and white linen robes, with mitres and shoes, curiously wrought and embroidered with gold. They lead a life of purity and delicacy, and attend chiefly the service of the gods. Here we have the Indian hierarchy of Diodorus Siculus. In the thirtieth page of Pliny's Natural History we also find matter equally relevant to the point in question; and even the doubts of Plutarch, in his treatise on Isis and Osiris, is a sort of conjectural confirmation of the colossal imagery and wonderful workmanship of Indian temples having then existed, after the worship of the divinity had by slow and silent steps decayed from the pure contemplation to symbolical objects, and emblematical devices created by the artifice of priests; it is therefore reasonable to suppose, that the passive pusillanimous Indian would soon become a dupe to the self-elected dispensers of eternal bliss, whose objects were exclusive thraldom; and nothing could be better adapted to influence a weak or timid race than the mystical images that are enshrined in gloom, and arrayed in all the horrors of demoniacal ferocity, in the cavern solitudes of Salsette and Elephanta.

Judicial astrology, with all the magical arts and incantations, were no doubt auxiliaries to the wily but scientific Brahmin; but the most seductive symbol of superstitious adoration seems to have been the Phallus.

The system of materialism to which it gave rise contaminated at a very remote era the pure stream of theism which then pervaded India; and, it would seem, the worship of nature, developed in the several impure emblems of the *Lingam* and *Yoni*, owes its origin to the Gymnosophists of India, and its diffusion over Babylonia, Egypt, Phœnicia, Syria, Greece, and Rome. Perhaps the tendency of this superstitious idolatry was, on its first promulgation in India, corrected by a severe morality, as the rites of Siva were twofold, and were propitiated with awful solemnity in the fanes of the dark and blood-stained Kali, as well as those of the more gross and sensual Siva. The vicissitude which nature was constantly undergoing, according to the Hindoo mythology, made therefore these obscene symbols be regarded in a sublime and spiritual sense; which soon degenerated into Bacchanalian revels when transplanted into other climes; gradually subverting all traces of the original doctrines of regeneration, until ending in the licentious feast of the Saturnalia, or the still more degrading mysteries of Eleusis. Such scenes of moral debasement never polluted the caves of Salsette or Elephanta; and offerings to the Lingam and Yoni, the types of creative power, are still made in these hallowed sanctuaries, freed from sensual ideas or impure emotions.

The unadorned fabric of Boodhaism, combined with the worship of the solar orb, I believe to have been the first heresy, and that the complicated worship of Siva, with all the monstrous attributes and meretricious ramifications which accompany it, are of more recent introduction. At all events, there is no reason to believe the benign religion of Bood'h, who is always represented absorbed in contemplation, and clothed with meekness, subordinate to a system of mythology that inculcated in every part the most chimerical forms of worship, and avows the most sanguinary and polluted ceremonies. A pure Boodhaic temple abounds with simple ornamental imagery. Nature is never perverted by the exhibitions of monsters, nor is it degraded by obscene personifications; and although the caves of Elephanta appear of more ancient formation than those of Amboli or Salsette, my opinion of the religion of Bood'h having existence at a period when the former was excavated is proved by his image being introduced among the celestial attendants of that temple, and in the same state of abstraction from sublunary objects as he is every where else met with. His woolly and frizzled hair, thick lips, and Herculean form, are cogent reasons for believing this shape of the divinity to have been of foreign importation. The aquiline or straight nose forms one objection to the generally received opinion of his being copied from the European, or African negro. But it is a curious fact, that the Devanpals, or hordes in the caves of Ibsambol in Nubia, have precisely the same appearance. The coincidence, in the sculptured details, of Egypt, Persia, and Hindoostan, are every where perceptible, and seem to have had one common origin.

BOODHAIC CAVE TEMPLES IN KANDEISH, AT THE BOTTOM OF THE AJUNTA GHAUT.

The first cave consists of an oblong portico, resting on round and fluted pillars of great strength and good proportions, having an apartment of a smaller size, with a recess fronting the entrance, containing a colossal figure of Bood'h, in a sitting and meditating posture; several smaller figures, appearing to be disciples or attendants, are grouped round the large one; near the feet, animals resembling deer, supporting the great image; and around the walls of the principal compartments various forms are sculptured in high relief, and all out of the solid rock, which is of a hard and durable nature, in colour and grain resembling basalt. There are small cells off the portico adjoining the recess; and the whole of the excavation is flat-roofed, and in good preservation.

The second is a small temple with a vaulted roof, and which, from the shape, and manner of cutting the arched parts of the rock into forms resembling ribs in naval architecture, has a striking likeness to the inverted bottom of a ship, to which it has been often compared. At the farthest end is a pyramidal building, supposed to contain some relic of the saint to whom the temple is sacred. It is not covered, as is usual, with the figure of an umbrella, but is crowned at top with squares, not unlike the inverted pedestals of pillars, three of three different sizes being placed one over the other, having the largest uppermost. In this and the next arched cave, which fell under our observation, the ribs do not appear in the body of the place, as they do in those of Canara, in the island of Salsette, and of Carli, about half way between Bombay and Poonah, but are seen in the aisles, about the height of the pillars from the floor of the cave.

The third corresponds in design with that of the one at Ellora, called the Carpenter's Cave, and in size pretty nearly with that of the great temple at Canara, being about one hundred and twenty feet long, forty feet broad, and from thirty to forty high, crowned like, and otherwise agreeing with that in No. 2, already described. In this mound, fronting the entrance, there is a niche, which at some former period may have contained an image, but at present it is empty, and we did not observe any sculptured figures in this or the other vaulted cave, with the exception of two small ones, near the upper parts of the entrance of No. 3, at the angles formed by the arch and the perpendiculars of the excavation. Figures of this kind were observed on several of the caves, and particularly over the parts near the entrances, and at the doorways, where they are placed in the same sort of positions, and apparently with the same sort of design, as cherubims are sometimes represented in European buildings.

The fourth cave is flat roofed, and of nearly a square form, of more than sixty feet to a side, and fifteen or sixteen feet high, having a kind of inner square formed by the rows of pillars that support the roof, some of which are fluted, a few are octagonal, and others round. A gigantic figure of Bood'h in one of the common attitudes, surrounded with the usual symbols, fills the recess fronting the door, which is guarded by huge *Darpals*, the doorway being very beautifully and tastefully carved.

The fifth, in size and general appearance, corresponds with, though it possesses more sculpture than, the fourth cave, having, among other figures, two colossal Bood'hs with all their accompaniments; and the paintings represented all over the walls, roofs, and pillars, are more entire than those of any other cave which we observed. There are paintings in all, and several of the scenes in the one under description are particularly well executed: these would appear to represent state processions, public ceremonies, and religious rites and observances; but the figures, whether of men and women, or of the brute creation, like the sculpture of the caves, are all human and natural.

The sixth cave is something like the one at Ellora named *Teen Lokh*, supposed to represent the three Boodhist divisions, of hell, earth, and heaven. But the two former stories having sunk in, or been filled up by the rocks and masses of the superincumbent mountain, that, loosened by the rain, or other causes, occasionally fall down, the upper part only is accessible. This, like the others, contains a colossal Bood'h, with all the usual smaller figures, and much fine painting, in a very perfect state, particularly at the entrances and over the portico, where some of the borders of these scenes, in arabesque, are highly ornamented, and remarkably neat and graceful. In the caves of Elephanta, Salsette, and Ellora, few remains of paintings can now be discovered, whilst almost every part of those at Leynapore appears to have been ornamented with paintings in fresco, and in a style so chaste, accurate, and natural, that one can hardly suppose them the work of Asiatic artists.

The seventh is a plain, flat roofed cave; and after what has been said of the fourth and fifth, which it in some respects resembles, does not require any particular description.

In the space which contains these seven, there were once several others, that are now filled up by the settling of the mountains, which, as the natives of the country say, in the instances alluded to, "Byth gye hyn." The masses of the rocks, above the roofs, are of great height and prodigious weight; and as the pillars appear to yield to the action of water, which oozes through the roof and settles in some of the caves, besides what must be driven in by the east and south winds during the rains, it is likely that such as are liable to injuries from these causes, though now tolerably entire, will soon become a heap of inaccessible ruins.

They are, for several reasons, highly deserving of the attention of the Indian mythologist, antiquary, and artist; and particularly so as they seem to have been designed and executed solely for the performance and exercise of the Boodhist rites and ceremonies, since they contain no intermixture whatever of the gods and emblems of the religion of the Brahmins and modern Hindoos *.

CHINRAI PUTTAN.

Forty miles north-west of the city of Seringapatam, the capital of Mysore, stands the town of Chinrai Puttan, or more properly speaking, Jeyne Rai Putun, i. e. the City of the Royal Jeyne Prince. The fort above, situated on an

* Calcutta Journal, 1818.

eminence, appears of considerable strength; in the niches of the walls are placed statues of Brahma, Vishnu, and Siva, the Indian triad. At a small distance from the fort, on the summit of a granite rock, half a mile high, and almost perpendicular in its ascent, stands the colossal figure of the supreme deity of the Jeynes, called *Gomuta Ishwara.* This rock is termed by the natives Indragurry, signifying the fort of Indra. The Indian god of the firmament on the summit is the statue before mentioned, and, on approaching, the beholder is struck with astonishment at the appearance of the enormous figure of black marble, completely naked, and standing in an erect posture, seventy feet in height; this figure, though of enormous bulk, is well proportioned, and the breadth and elevation of his shoulders are much admired. He stands on the Lotus; and near the base of the pedestal are large slabs of marble, on which Jeyne characters are inscribed in the Canara language. Before this immense image are two other figures, about five feet high, representing dancing girls; an appendage which is constantly attached to the images of their Dewtahs throughout Hindoostan. In a veranda or gallery which runs through the whole are the images of the twenty-four incarnations of the divinity, according to the Jeyne ritual. What is remarkable in the construction of this stupendous figure is, that it is cut out of the solid rock of granite on which it stands, and it bears not the least appearance of any part of the enormous mass having been joined to the others. Opposite to this stupendous rock of granite is a small hill, called *Chandragurus,* on which are to be seen, amidst an assemblage of Jeyne Dewtahs, the print of two immense feet, recorded by tradition as the feet of Parus Nauth Ishwara, the great Jeyne patriarch, who, it is said, taking a spring from this place, flew up to heaven, and was absorbed in the divine essence. In various other parts of the eastern world are to be seen similar impressions, and the *Paduka,* or holy feet of Jeyne and Bood'h, have in a later age been attributed by his followers to the arch impostor Mahomed *.

It is evident, then, from these remains near the city of Chinrai Puttan, that it must, at a remote period, have been

* They are termed in India, Persia, and Arabia, *Cuddum Rusool,* or the Prophet's Foot.—Author.

the capital of a Jeyne empire of very great extent. I am inclined to suppose it existed in Southern India, about the period of the invasion of Alexander the Great, whose conference with the Jeyne philosopher Dindamis has been noticed by various authors, both ancient and modern *.

The expulsion of the Jeynes and Boodhists by the modern Brahmins, which took place about one thousand years since, is one of the strongest proofs of the priority of the Jeyne worship over that of the modern Brahmins; and notwithstanding the bloody persecutions that followed that event, the Jeynes, even to the present day, are numerous throughout Hindoostan; and their worship, collated and compared with that of the Boodhists, with very slight variations, is, in fact, one and the same thing; and obtains, at the present moment, from Bootan to China, and the numerous shores of the Indian archipelago. Bood'h, in fact, is no other than the great transmigrating father, the patriarch Noah, which sufficiently demonstrates the antiquity of his worship †.

* Palladius de Gentibus Indiæ.

† Faber, passim.

BHILSA.

From the kingdom of Mysore we advance again up the peninsula, and, after crossing the Nerbuddah river, enter the fertile province of Malwah, and the town of Bhilsa. In the neighbourhood of that town are the remains of various Jeyne temples, too remarkable to be passed over in a discussion like the present *.

Four miles distant from Bhilsa, on a table land, is an ancient temple, of hemispherical form. It is of freestone without cement, and to all appearance solid, and the measured circumference of the whole is five hundred and fifty-four feet. A colonnade of granite pillars surrounds the building. They are ten feet in height, and distant from each other a foot and a half; it forms a spacious veranda. The east, west, and north faces present the highest gateways, one of which is forty

* I shall here avail myself of the labours of the lamented Captain Fell, of the Bengal infantry, and give an outline of what he has detailed, in a masterly manner, in the Calcutta Journal and in the Asiatic Researches.

feet high; and the lintels of these gateways are adorned with sculptured elephants. In every part of this noble building are to be seen groups of figures, both male and female, of elegant sculpture, some of which is said to resemble the Grecian costume, more especially in the graceful folds of the drapery of the females *. On entering the principal gateway is a statue of Bood'h as large as life, of dark basalt. He is seated cross-legged, on a throne supported by four lions couchant, and attendants are observed on both sides of the throne, fanning the divinity with chowries, or Indian fly-flappers. The door-keepers at the entrance of the temple are armed with maces, and have helmets on their heads. In another part of the interior are observed groups of figures in the act of worshipping the sacred tree called *Kulbirj*, and an altar in front. But above all, the most singular is one bearing a manifest allusion to the universal Deluge. A boat is seen, the prow

* A similar remark has been made by Belzoni and others, especially regarding the female figures and sculptured memorial of the Deluge from the Jeyne temple at Bhilsa. See Captain Fell's Account of the Jeyne Temples at Bhilsa, in the Asiatic Researches.

of which is a lion's head, and the stern has the expanded tail of a fish, over which is wound a cable. The boat is surmounted by a square canopy of carved work, supported by two pillars. Within the canopy are seated two figures; one holding an umbrella, the other a chowrie; and at the stern is a third figure steering the boat. The vessel is on an open sea, in the midst of a tempest; near it are seen figures struggling in the water, and endeavouring, by seizing large piles, and other things, to save themselves from sinking. One, in particular, on the point of drowning, is making an expiring effort to ascend the side of the vessel; and the features of the whole group sufficiently portray their melancholy situation *.

The upper parallels of this costly temple, says Captain Fell, are beautifully sculptured with hooded serpents, passing through them in spiral wreaths. In a spacious chamber which faces the eastern entrance, the roof of which is flat, and supported by a double row of pilasters of granite, is a gigantic Jeyne statue, the profile of the face measuring thirteen inches

* Plate I.

TESTIMONIALS OF THE DELUGE FROM THE TEMPLES AT BHILSAH.

from the fore curls of his woolly head to the chin; but the nose and lips of this figure have been disfigured by the hand of bigotry, and the arms are broken off below the elbows; a circumstance which occurs in almost every Jeyne figure that is discovered by the curious.

On projecting pedestals of the chamber are small figures of Parus Nauth Ishwara, sitting cross-legged; and in a corner of the same apartment is another figure of Parus Nauth, over whose head are five expanded serpents' hoods, the distinguishing mark of this Jeyne patriarch throughout Hindoostan.

From Bhilsa, taking an easterly direction, we come to Gurrah Mundala, in the country of the Berar rajah. Eight miles west of Ghurnah is a flat roofed Jeyne temple, the interior of which consists of a small central chamber, with a veranda all around. It is lighted only from a narrow doorway in front. The outer wall is lined with a row of Jeyne idols of Parus Nauth, in the usual sitting posture, with appropriate attendants on each side, standing erect. The walls are adorned with various figures sculptured in relievo; and after having witnessed, in various parts of the peninsula, the impure and obscene figures found in the temples of the modern Brahmins, the mind of the spectator is relieved by the chasteness of the Jeyne idols, which (though many of them are in a state of nature) do not excite disgust.

In the town of Belhari, distant from Saugor about thirty miles westward, are many Jeyne families who trace their descent to about six centuries backwards, and near the above mentioned town is a celebrated place of Jeyne worship, called Koondulpore, situated on the summit of a lofty hill, which contains from twelve to fifteen Jeyne temples, and an image of Parus Nauth Ishwara of gigantic dimensions, besides many other images of a smaller size.

The independent Rajpoot principality of *Sirookhi** is situated between the twenty-fourth and twenty-sixth degrees of

* For this account I am indebted to the kindness of my friend Captain Neufville, of the quarter-master-general's establishment in Bengal.—Author.

north latitude, and the seventy-second and seventy-fourth of east longitude: it is bounded on the north by Maridar and Godewar; on the west by the Little Desert; on the south by Pakranpoor; and on the east by the Arabulla mountains, which divide it from the Oodipoor territory and the province of Maywar. The principal streams are the Bunass, flowing from the more eastern quarter, and the Seip from the central: these unite at the north-western limit, and flow to the sea. Numerous Nullahs also intersect every part of the country, of which the most remarkable are the Kissnavutte and the Juwace. The soil is rich, and vegetation luxuriant; and, with the exception of the more hilly parts, the whole territory might, without doubt, be brought into the highest state of agricultural improvement. The government is absolute; and, like all uncivilized states, depending for support on its own physical strength less than hereditary opinion, or the existence of any moral compact or mutual obligation between the ruler and the subject. The present dynasty has, with the usual proportion of despotism and murder, occupied the throne during a period of seven hundred years. It is a branch of the Chouhan Rajpoots, originally from Jhalour sect, who now bear the name of Deora, in allusion to a family legend. The prince is styled Rao, and holds a respectable footing amongst the other great Rajpoot rulers, intermarrying with their families on equal grounds, or grounds influenced by pecuniary circumstances and relative political importance. The mode of government, and the power of the Rao, have always been subject to alteration and instability, depending chiefly on the crown resources, the character of the ruler and his relation with the neighbouring states, opposed to the power and influence of his great vassals, or feudal aristocracy, who, in many cases, have proved far too potent for the control of their lord paramount, and, in not a few, have altogether subverted the throne. Their lands are held in Jaghire or military tenure of service, which is rendered, or otherwise, in proportion to the ability of resistance to the orders and authority of the Rao. The revenue of the Rao *was* derived from the Khalsa or crown lands, in the first instance, and also by a general exaction levied on every town in the territory by arbitrary assessment, and generally proportioned rather to the necessities of the ruler than the ability of the people. The Rajpoots, however, of all ranks, were exempt from contribution, and the burden was made to fall upon the Bunyahs, Rewarrie merchants, and, in short, all who were known or suspected to have the means of supply. A Cheera ki Chithee, when served upon the town of one of the Taccoors, was always doubled in amount by him, and the excess carried to his private account, or the whole retained in case of weakness on the part of the Rao, and inability to maintain his rights. No other law appears to have existed in Siroohi than that of strength to govern the higher powers, or those of tyranny and arbitrary power over the great body of the people. This is divided into two distinct classes; the Rajpoot conquerors, who are, as in the old regime of France, a privileged order; and the mass of artisans, cultivators, &c. &c. composing the bulk of the community. The former have always exercised an iron sway over the latter, which they have submitted to till now without complaint or remonstrance. In addition to all these evils affecting the lower and more industrious class, they have been exposed, throughout every part of the territory, to ravage and plunder from numerous hordes of barbarians, abounding in the hilly region northward and eastward, and on the border of the desert on the opposite boundary. Of these the principal are, or were, the Meenahs, a raoe resembling the *Sicarii of Josephus*, who inhabited the holes and fastnesses of a mass of hills in the northern quarter. These plunderers have, for many years, been the terror and scourge of Siroohi, and have defied all attempts, on the part of the state, to repress their ravages. Of late years they have exacted black mail, or a fourth (chowt) produce from almost the whole country, while a resistance to their demands has long been deemed a matter of impossibility by the once brave Rajpoots. The eastern hills, running back to the Arabulla range, are occupied by an equally predatory tribe of Bheels and Grasseahs; while to the southward the Kolee chiefs, and other marauders, were regular in their visitations of foray subsequent to every harvest. To all this is to be added a yearly invasion, or Moolkgeeree collection, by their powerful neighbours of Joudpoor, and an eternal scene of civil strife and internal dissension, either of Taccoors amongst themselves, or collectively against the authority of the Rao. It is needless to

Drawn on Stone by G. Scharf from a Sketch by Captn Newfville. Printed by C. Hullmandel.

Ancient Slab of Marble Built into the Wall of a modern Jeyne Temple at Sirohi.

add, that the country was found to be in the utmost state of anarchy and confusion. The religious knowledge of the Siroohi people is of the most confined nature, and indeed their ignorance on every topic is at the lowest ebb. The Brahminical worship is almost universally appropriated to Bhawani, and Seeva, and generally of a deprecatory nature. No temples of the Brahminical deities are found, either extant or in ruin, which exhibit signs of architectural beauty or magnificence; but the want of that is amply atoned for by those of the Jeynes, which abound in all the towns and villages, all of solid and excellent structure, and some of surpassing beauty and costly design. Of these last, the most remarkable are situated at Dilwara, on the summit of the holy mountain of Aboo or Arbooa, in the midst of the Siroohi state, which were erected about six hundred years ago, and are still nearly perfect. They are built entirely of white marble, sculptured throughout in the most exquisite and elaborate manner, and combining richness of execution with a degree of elegance and taste seldom met with in native buildings. The beauty of the roofs and domes, with their deep pendants, defies all description.

These temples are all dedicated to Parus Nauth, whose image, of colossal dimensions, of white marble, occupies the sacred fanes. Figures of Neem Nath, of gigantic size, of black marble or basalt, with the curly hair and Ethiopian features, are also to be seen occasionally, though the prevailing contour of their countenances is with the aquiline nose. The curly head, however, is universal. South-eastward of Siroohi are some similarly splendid fabrics at Amta Bawarri. These were all, it is said, erected by the merchants of Puttun, a city about a hundred miles to the southward, whose descendants still continue to defray the expenses of the worship. This is performed by orthodox Brahmins, the Juttees having all quitted a land so drowned in blood as Siroohi.

PARUS NAUTH.

From Saugor, taking a north-easterly direction, we traverse the province of Berar; and continuing our course in route, in the same parallel, advance to the frontiers of *Behar*, or *Maj-*

hada, and the Bhaugulpore district, the ancient dominions of Sandracottus, sovereign of Palibothra, and of the Prasu and Gangarides. At the foot of the mountain Parus Nauth, on the Rham Ghur frontier, and a hundred and thirty-six miles south of Bhaugulpore, are situated the temples dedicated to Parus Nauth Ishwara, the twenty-third deified saint of the Jeynes, and one of the principal places of the Jeynes' worship in Hindoostan: they consist of large square brick buildings, painted white, with a dome in the centre, and four smaller domes at the four corners; the centre dome is crowned with a gilded spire, like the Piathas of the Bood'haic temples of Ava, as described by Colonel Symes.

The domes of all the temples are surmounted by cullises of copper gilt, which shine like burnished gold. In front of each temple or *Mundala* is a Nobut Khana, or gallery for music, the instruments of which are constantly playing during the time of worship. A brick wall surrounds the whole, and at the end is a dhurrumsala, or sarai, for the use of visitors and worshippers. Within the area of the largest of these temples we were eye-witnesses of a poojah, or worship performed at the temple. On a chabootra, or terrace, was a square *Sameanah*, or canopy of white cloth, below which was another smaller one of rich brocade, supported by four red painted poles; on an elevated throne, covered with brocade, and called by the natives *Singhausan*, was seated a small black stone figure of Parus Nauth, sitting cross-legged, with his hands before him; on his head, fashioned like a turban, were seven expanded heads of serpents, the Cobra de Capella, or hooded snake of India, the invariable symbol of Parus Nauth; below his feet were placed flowers of the double marigold; and a small silver umbrella was placed erect before him; underneath the umbrella incense was burning, and great quantities of marigolds scattered about the place; at the sides of the throne were placed plantains, cocoa nuts, the Paun or betle-leaf, and many other kinds of fruits, as offerings to the deity. The two officiating priests had cloths tied round their mouth and underneath the chin *, which was fastened to the top of

* The holy fire, says the editor of the Oriental Magazine, amongst the Persians was kept alive day and night by the priests on the altar within the temple.

the head, for fear of their swallowing any thing that had life; the other two priests wore plain *chaders* or sheets, and were standing. On a high teapoy, or tripod, were placed the *pooties* or extracts from the Puranas, which they chanted aloud. The two head priests were sitting on the ground, the others standing, and all four singing in praise of Parus Nauth. The ceremony was performed in the area of the temple; the priests sounded the conch, and played on cymbals, and before the figure they burnt incense, and sung hymns to his praise. When the priest sounded the conch, one of the others offered three flags, called by the natives Sathica *, on a brass plate to Parus Nauth, upon which he put all kinds of perfumes, and then the whole band in the Noobut Khana struck up. From sun-rise

At times of worship the priest puts on a white robe and mitre with a gauze covering before his mouth, that he might not breathe on the sacred element. This resemblance is striking.—AUTHOR.

* Thus: 

Agreeably to the Jeyne tenets, these flags bear the following meanings.

No. 1. Gyau, knowledge.

No. 2. Dursun, a sight of the divinity.

No. 3. Churriter, worshippers of Parus Nauth.

to sun-set you hear nothing but the incessant din of their harsh and discordant music.

The ascent to Parus Nauth mountain commences by a narrow path in a winding direction, surrounded on both sides by the thickest forest; it is pretty steep, with loose stones overspreading the road. As you proceed the ascent becomes steeper, and the summit of the mountain in front presents a stupendous appearance. The course up is due south; no animal of any kind is to be seen. On an opening of the forest you gain an extensive view of the Jungle Terry, and the temples at the bottom are seen to advantage. After passing over some level ground between the two hills, you again ascend, and shortly after complete the first range of this extraordinary mountain; proceed on, over elevated ground; commence a descent, which brings you to the foot of the second range; pass along the banks of the Ghundraup Nullah, which runs in the bottom over its rocky bed, in loud and sonorous murmurs, amidst the gloom of a deep glen, and arched over-head with umbrageous foliage; the road continues through the forest till you reach the Ghundraup Nullah, which you cross, and commence the ascent to the second range; after crossing you continue to ascend. On the right is seen a large block of quartz rock, covered over with sindoor or red lead and oil, and dedicated to Ghundraup, the presiding deity of the place. The ascent continues, and the forest begins to thin; we are now at a very high elevation, and distinctly hear the roarings of the Seeta river in the bottom. The road continues in a winding direction, and, at intervals, you perceive the summits of Parus Nauth appearing in bluff jagged peaks, eight in number, and towering to the clouds; commence a descent, which brings you to the Seeta river in a bottom, rolling over a bed of large misshapen rocks. On the right is a figure of Hanuman, and on the left a small temple, dedicated to Seeta, the wife of Rama. After crossing the rocky bed of the Seeta river, whose waters are cool and clear as crystal, you commence the ascent to the third range, which is far more difficult than the two former, and, in some parts, nearly perpendicular; the road being covered with large stones from a foot and a half to two feet high, over the tops of which you are obliged to pass with great hazard of your life. At this part of the ascent, though seated in a small *dooly*, or chair, in a cramped position, it took twenty bearers to carry me over these stones,—so insecure to the footing, that a false step would have precipitated the whole of the party over an abyss, on the right, of between three and four hundred feet in depth, into the valley below. Gain an opening in the forest, from which the view is inexpressibly grand, the wide extent of the Jungle Terry appearing as if beneath your feet, and looking like the surface of a pictured landscape. With very great difficulty we at length reached the summit, from which the view is difficult to describe, as by this time a thick haze nearly covered the atmosphere, the result of a strong south-west wind, which blew all the way up; otherwise I can have no hesitation in supposing, that the view would have equalled any thing ever witnessed. I tried, by means of a telescope, to discover the mountain Tyoor, and perhaps Maudar, but owing to the haze was disappointed. On the plain, however, I could discover the course of five or six rivers which intersect this part of the Jungle Terry. The coup d'œil upon the whole, though clouded, was magnificent.

The summit, emphatically termed by the Jeynes *Asmeed*

Drawn on Stone by [illegible] | [illegible]

SOUTH VIEW OF THE JEYNE TEMPLES AT PARUS NAUTH MOUNTAIN.

From a Drawing by Sir C. Doyley Bar.t

Sikur, or "the Peak of Bliss," composes a table land, flanked by twenty small Jeyne temples, situate on the craggy peaks, and in different parts of the mountain.

These temples, in shape, very much resemble an extinguisher; in them is to be seen the Vasu Padukas, or the sacred feet, as is seen in the Jeyne temple at Chumpanuggur, and has been before described in the first part of Palibothra.

The figure of Parus Nauth is in the temple below: but on the south side of the mountain, about half way down, is a large and very handsome flat roofed temple, which contains several figures of the deity; which exhibit the never-failing attributes of Parus Nauth and the Jeyne religion, viz. the crowned serpent and the cross-legged figures of Jeyne Ishura, or Jeyne the preserver and guardian of mankind*. So difficult is the access to this mountain, that people ascend by means of a very small dooly carried by four bearers: they are for hire at the village below, called Muddhobund. The fixed

* This mountain, agreeably to road travelling, is six English miles from the base to the summit, but not a continued ascent.

price is five rupees for the ascent and descent of the mountain, and it takes them a whole day: as they stop to perform their ablutions and offerings to the temples, they often do not reach the village till late at night. The road is so difficult that the bearers can only undertake the journey every fourth day *.

PUTTERGHOTTA.

In the fabulous æra of the Sutta Jog, or golden age of the Hindoos, there reigned at Benares, or Cashee, a celebrated Rajah, named *Devi Dassa*, who, after performing *Tapashya*, or abstracted mental devotion, was gratified by the appearance of Mahadeva and his consort Parvati: they expressed their

* It is here necessary to remark, that the foregoing account of the Parus Nauth mountain was presented to the Royal Asiatic Society when the Author was as yet undetermined as to publishing the whole of his Researches on the Tenets and Doctrines of the Jeynes and Boodhists; but circumstances more favourable to the publication having recently occurred, he trusts that the public will not attribute improper motives to him, in sending forth to the world a double statement of the same thing. *Liceat repetisse!*—Author.

satisfaction at his devotions, and commanded him to signify his wishes. The Rajah requested the kingdom of Cashi, or Benares: Mahadeva granted his demand, and gave him the kingdom of Cashi; after which he repaired, with his consort Parvati, to the mountain Kailas (Paradise), both much grieved that they had parted with Cashi. "Alas!" exclaimed Mahadeva, "where shall we find another Cashi?" Mahadeva then, after expressing his grief (*paraite*) *, said, "Let us seek out another Cashi, in lieu of that which passed away, and another Kailas, or Paradisaical mountain." They accordingly roamed through the earth; they passed to Kemalah, or Kimanchul, in the bowels of which mountain were mines of gold, and its summit was covered with everlasting snows; from thence, grieved that their object was not obtained, Mahadeva and his consort passed to Mount Meru, (the North Pole). This mountain is of a cylindrical form, and the highest in the world.

* This account is taken from the fifteenth Adhyayeh or section of the Vaya Puraun.

The sun here rises from the gorge, or pass through the mountain, which is cleft in two. Here resided all the Dewtahs, or celestial beings; here was erected *Vicontha*, the abode of Vishnu, and above it the summit of Kailas, or Paradise. Still unsatisfied as to the object of their research, they circumambulated the world, and at last arrived at Ghuree Soondur, "the beautiful abode," or Putterghotta hill, at the south side of which the Ganges is joined to the hill, and is therefore denominated *Sillah Sungum*, or the junction of the river with the rocks. The neighbouring plains are beautiful and surpassingly fertile; on its sides and summit are caverns, in which the divinity is worshipped: the inhabitants of these caves lead a solitary and recluse life.

The river here runs due north for about nine miles. This place, then, Mahadeva pronounced to be a second Cashi, and ordered worship to be performed there. On the north side of the river, near its opposite bank, is the confluence of the Cosi with the Ganges. Finally, the Supreme Being having, at this place, been manifested from a *buttie*, or bur-tree, the mountain received the appellation for ever of Butteeshur, or the Hill of the Divine Tree*. So celebrated is the worship performed at this place, and so great is its efficacy, that any one who has performed his devotions at Butteeshur, the whole of his desires will be gratified, and the favour of the Supreme Being be obtained†. Having already spoken of the excavated chambers at Putterghotta in the fourth part of my essay on Palibothra, I shall here briefly remark, that these chambers are stated, by the learned Dr. Tytler, to be of a similar nature in their construction and use as those to be seen in the Brambanan, a mountain on the island of Java, dedicated to Bood'h, which plainly evinces a similarity of worship having obtained in the two places, and those at Putterghotta were doubtless in use at the period of the dominion of the royal dynasty of Bali, in the imperial city of Palibothra. The annexed engraving of the principal chamber, called *Bedieoosurung*, or chamber of

* Might it not be Bood'h Ishwara, or Bood'h the supreme, the hill Buteeshir, or Bood'h-Ishwara combined?

† In the month of Maug, or January, a vast assemblage of pilgrims from all parts of India resort to the hill Buteeshir, for the purpose of performing *poojah*, and bathing in the Ganges at the Sillah Sungum. Several temples have, of late years, been erected in the neighbourhood of Cashidie or Putterghotta.—AUTHOR.

knowledge, will contribute to illustrate the description of that place, as already given in my essay *.

ISLAND OF JAVA, IN THE EASTERN ARCHIPELAGO.

I cannot quit India, on this interesting subject, without a few remarks on the Boodhaic temples to be seen in the island of Java in the Indian Archipelago; and here I shall principally follow the account of the Boodhaic relics to be there found, as

* Shortly after writing the above, I paid a third visit to Putterghotta and the hill Buteeshur. The ascent is in a winding direction, over large loose stones. In the course of the ascent you come to five different chambers, cut out of the solid rock; and the hill is occasionally interspersed with trees and verdure. The principal chamber, called *Bedieoosurung*, or chamber of knowledge, is on the north side of the hill, and is cut out of the solid rock. It is one hundred and thirty-six feet in length, twenty-four in breadth, and twelve feet in height, without a beam or pillar of any kind to support the enormous mass; and may, I think, be considered as one of the most curious caverns in India. At the upper end is a separate small chamber, apart from the rest of the cave, which most probably formed the *sacellum*, or sanctuary, for the purpose of worship. There is nothing whatever in the cave. From the summit of the hill you have a fine view of the mouth of the Cosi river, on the opposite bank, flowing into the Ganges from the north.—Bhaugulpore, 1822.

detailed by Mr. Crawford in his excellent History of the Indian Archipelago.

In the island of Java, the most considerable and perfect remains of the temples of the first class are afforded in the ruins of Brambana, situated partly in the district of Pajang, and partly in that of Mataram. Among the many groups of temples here to be traced is that termed by the natives of the country, "the thousand temples *." The whole group occupies an area, which is an oblong square of six hundred English feet long, and five hundred and fifty broad.

It consists of four rows of small temples, inclosing in the centre a greater one, whose height is sixty feet. The temples are pyramidal buildings all of the same character, covered by a profusion of sculpture, and consisting of large blocks of hewn stone. Each of the smaller temples contained a figure of Buddha, and the great central one, consisting of several apartments, figures of the principal objects of worship, which have consisted of the destroying power of the Hindoo triad, or of some of his family. To the whole group

* Crawford's Indian Archipelago.

of temples there are four entrances, facing the cardinal points of the compass, and each is guarded by two gigantic statues, as warders, measuring, in a kneeling posture, not less than nine feet and a half, and being, in girth, full eleven feet.

The temple of Boro Budur, or more properly speaking, Boro Bood'h, the Great Bood'h, situated in the mountainous and romantic land of Kadu, is a square building of a pyramidal shape, ending in a dome. It embraces the summit of a small hill, rising perpendicularly from the plain, and consists of a series of six square walls, with corresponding terraces; three circular rows of latticed cages of hewn stone in the form of bee-hives. The height of the whole building is about one hundred and sixteen feet, and at the base each side measures in extent five hundred and twenty-six English feet. There is no concavity except in the dome. The hill is, in fact, a sort of nucleus for the temple, and has been cut away and fashioned for the accommodation of the buildings. The outer and inner side of each wall is covered with a profusion of sculpture, and in various situations are niches containing figures of Bood'h, amounting in all to between three and four hundred.

To the temple of Boro Budur * there are four entrances, facing the cardinal points; but here, instead of the monstrous figures in human shape, we have lions as warders †.

At Suku, probably Saca, is another place of worship in the island of Java ‡, the principal structure of which is a truncated pyramid, situated on the most elevated of three successive terraces. The ruins of two obelisks, having the form of the section of a pyramid, are also observable in the vicinity of the principal building, and on each side of the western front appear several piles of ruinous buildings and sculpture. The length of the terraces is about one hundred and fifty-seven feet; the depth of the first, eighty feet, of the second, thirty, and of the highest, one hundred and thirty feet.

The approach is from the west, through three porches or gateways, of which the outermost alone is now standing. This gateway is about sixteen feet high, of a pyramidal form. The

* Tytler, Boro Bood'h.

† The lion is to be seen in every species of Hindoo worship; the Durga of the modern Hindoos rides upon one.

‡ Raffles's History of Java.

entrance is seven feet and a half high, and about three feet wide. A gorgon's head forms the key-stone of the arch. On the outer face of the gateway several figures are sculptured in relief. On the right side of the principal figure is that of a man of monstrous appearance devouring a child. On his right hand a dog sitting, the head of which is wanting; a bird of the stork kind, near the root of a tree, on one of the branches of which a bird not unlike a dove or pigeon is perched; over the figure is a bird on the wing; either the hawk or eagle. Above is the figure of a man, with the tail of a snake writhing in his mouth; another appeared to be that of a sphinx. It is represented as floating in the air, as is seen in the ruins of Persepolis, with the legs, arms, and tail extended; the tail is similar to that of the lizard species, and the hands appear to be webbed claws; but the body, limbs, and face are human; the breasts distinguished it as a female. Over this, again, is a small curling reptile, like a worm or small snake, reminding us of the asp. On the north and south face of the gateway there is a colossal eagle with extended wings, holding in its talons an immense serpent plaited in three folds, its head turned towards the eagle, and ornamented with a coronet. It is impossible to reflect on the design of these sculptures without being forcibly struck with their similarity to the ancient monuments of Egypt. The form of the gateway itself, and of all the ruins within view, was pyramidal. In the monster devouring the child, we are reminded of Typhon, an emblem of the deluge: the tree seemed to be the palm, by which the Egyptians designated the year; the pigeon, the hawk, and the immense serpents, were all symbols of Egyptian worship.

Amongst other figures to be seen at this temple is one of the woolly-headed, thick-lipped, long-eared, cross-legged Bood'h, similar in its features to those of Ava, Siam, Canara, Ceylon, Japan, and other Boodhaic countries, as well as in the Brahminical region of the Dekhan.

Speaking of figures in the same ruins, Captain Baker observes, that on reaching the southern face of the temple of Chandi Siv, you find yourself suddenly opposed by two gigantic figures, in a kneeling posture, and of terrific forms; both armed with clubs of enormous bulk. But the most extraordinary appendage of these porters is a very large full-bottomed wig, in full curl, all of which, the Brahmins assured Captain Baker, were intended to represent the usual mode observed by the Moonee, or saints, to dress their natural hair *.

We find here, then, a very strong collateral proof of the extent of the Bood'h or Jeyne faith, throughout the great island of Sumatra, which, coupled with the details before exhibited of the fact respecting the Bengal sepoys when in Egypt, the striking similitude of the Jeynes of the islands of the Indian archipelago with those of continental India and Egypt, and the diffusion of the Boodhaic or Jeyne faith, over Ceylon, Siam, Ava, and to the extremities of Japan and China, —all these links connected together sufficiently establish the priority of the Jeyne religion over that of modern Brahminism. It evidently points out the Boodhaic or Jeyne doctrines to have obtained in the remotest ages of creation †.

* Sir T. Raffles's History of Java.

† The French sçavans who accompanied Buonaparte into Egypt talk of "blowing off Memnon's wig."—Denon.

JEYNE & BOOD'H FIGURES IN SUMATRA.

PERSIA.

If we advance to the widely-extended region of Persia, we shall find that most of the temples in that interesting country were caverns in the rocks, either formed by nature or artificially produced; over and above which they had fire-temples, the *Puratheia* of the Greeks, for the celebration of the worship of fire. These, in the opinion of the learned Bryant, were the works also of the Cuthites, descendants of Chus, the son of Ham, whose magnificent erections have so frequently been spoken of in the course of this discussion. Amongst others are the very curious monuments to be seen both at Persepolis and Nukshi Rustom, where the worship of fire and cavern worship combined are to be seen in the numerous excavated chambers in both those places. It is no less remarkable that one of these buildings, described by Hyde *, bears a striking resemblance to the temple at Luxor, in Upper Egypt; a most

* That called the tomb of Darius Hystaspes; a plate of which is to be seen in Kæmpfer.

striking coincidence of a similarity of worship obtaining in both countries at a very remote period.

The caverns and fire-temples of Persia have been so frequently described by different travellers, that it is useless to enter into a detail of them in this place: but I may be excused for remarking, that after a lapse of more than thirty years, I find my conjectures on the subject of the fire-worship at Persepolis, made in very early youth, confirmed; for which I am thankful to the Author of all good.

I shall here add another observation, namely, that memorials of the deluge are visible in various parts of these noble ruins, at Persepolis, at Darab, and at Nakhshi Rostum *, where the dark excavated chamber, and the narrow door at the entrance of each, exhibit a memorable allusion to the ship of the deluge, as wedged in the crags of mount Ararat, after traversing the pathless tracts of the great waters of the general deluge; whilst the solitary and unadorned state of the chambers within present an admirably correct picture of the gloom and solitude

* Sir William Ouseley's Travels in Persia, vol. ii. article Persepolis.

of the ark, the abode of the great transmigrating father of mankind, the patriarch Noah and his family, consisting of that celebrated *ogdoad* so well known in after ages throughout the Pagan world.

In the country of the Afghans many remarkable monuments of antiquity are found, consisting of chambers, temples, and columns hewn out of the rocks, resembling the vast excavations which exist in India. Those, in particular, in the city of Bamiyan, eight days' journey from Cabul, are better known than the rest; in the territory of the before mentioned city, twenty thousand such caverns are reckoned up, and their number alone proves that they were the abodes, not of the dead, but the living; and were doubtless the dwellings of the *Hylobii* of Arrian, and Quintus Curtius; and, as these remains all bear the stamp of an Indian origin, we may justly ascribe them to the votaries of Bood'h, who has already been identified with the Mithras of Persia *.

The origin of the revival of the doctrines of Zeratusht, or

* Annals of Oriental Literature.

Zoroaster, or fire worship, is thus singularly accounted for in the Ardaviraf Nameh, or the Revelations of Ardaviraf, translated by Mr. Pope of Bombay *.

Ardeshir Babegan, king of Persia, having settled the Persian monarchy by conquering the provinces, and being also desirous to establish the national religion in its wonted purity, collected together all the priests, doctors, and others of the Magian religion, to the amount of forty thousand, whom he addressed as follows: "The revolution caused by the invasion of Alexander having destroyed the evidences of our holy religion, it is my wish that proper persons should be selected from your number, to collate and collect the laws left us by our prophet Zeratusht, that we may follow his laws, and get rid of the heresies that have been from time to time introduced; for this purpose let a selection be made out of your number, that this desirable object may be obtained." According to the king's order, four thousand were selected out of the forty thousand, which were

* Ardeshir Babegan was the fifth in descent from Darab, or Darius II.; and commenced his reign about the two hundred and second year of the Christian era.

subsequently reduced to four hundred, and afterwards to forty. A still further selection was then made, and seven only of the forty remained; these were men of the most holy lives without blemish: they were taken before the king, who explained to them his wishes, with respect to restoring the true religion of Zoroaster to its ancient purity. These holy persons, to the number of six, having selected one of their own body, *Ardaviraf* then informed the king, that he was the person who would carry his majesty's wishes into execution. The king being well pleased at this determination, accompanied these holy persons, together with the remainder of the forty thousand priests, and his whole court, to the principal temple of fire, and joined with them in devout prayer. Ardaviraf, having then performed the usual ablutions, and clothed himself in white, according to the rites of the Magian religion, presented himself in an attitude of prayer before the sacred fire *.

* Then follows the vision that ensued, and a narrative of the heaven and hell of the Persians; from which the Arabian impostor afterwards largely borrowed.

EGYPT.

Ancient Egypt consisted of a narrow region, which reached from Syene in Ethiopia, downwards to the Delta, following the course of the Nile. It is bounded on the east by the Red Sea and the Isthmus of Suez; on the south by Ethiopia; on the west by Libya; and on the north by the Mediterranean. The Nile runs from south to north through the whole country, six hundred miles in length. This long tract is inclosed on each side with a ridge of mountains. The space between the river and the hills, on either hand, sometimes extends only to the distance of sixteen miles. On the coast of the Mediterranean, the extent of the plain is above three hundred miles.

Ancient Egypt was divided into three principal parts: Upper Egypt, otherwise called Thebais, the most southern division; Middle Egypt, or Heptanomis, so called from the seven districts into which it was divided; and Lower Egypt, which included the Delta, and all the country as far as the

Red Sea, and along the Mediterranean to Rhinocolura, or Mount Casius. Under Sesostris all Egypt became one kingdom, and was divided into thirty-six governments. The cities of Syene and Elephantina divided Egypt from Ethiopia, and in the days of Augustus were the boundaries of the Roman Empire. This celebrated country had a claim to the attention of all nations and ages. The Egyptians were the first enlightened and refined people of the ancient world, and the specimens which they exhibited in arts and in literature became models of imitation to other nations. Here philosophy found its earliest seat, and the light of science was kindled, whose radiance diffusing itself over Greece, has successively illuminated the rest of the world. The wisdom of the Egyptians was proverbial among the nations of antiquity. Orpheus and Homer adopted their mythology; Pythagoras and Plato instructed themselves in their mathematical and philosophical discoveries; Lycurgus and Solon studied the principles of their legislation and government. When Greece was in the meridian of its splendour, and renowned for arts as well as arms, no person could rise to distinction who had not visited the banks of the Nile, and conversed with the fathers of science *.

Egypt was the mother of the sciences as well as the arts. An order of men, like the priests, devoted to study and contemplation, had a favourable opportunity to make discoveries, and to investigate truth. There were four colleges in Egypt, where science was studied and taught: Thebes, which Pythagoras visited; Memphis, where Thales and Democritus consulted the Egyptian priests; Heliopolis, where Plato studied; and Sais, where Solon was instructed in the principles of legislation and government. It is believed by the learned †, that there has existed a most intimate connexion between India and Egypt, and that colonies emigrating from Egypt to India, or vice versa, transported their deities into the countries where they took up their respective abodes; but which of these two nations first migrated is the question so frequently asked: I should be inclined to give the preference to Egypt, having given her gods to India, as she un-

* Rutherford's Ancient History, p. 10 and 12, 8vo edition.

† Maurice's Indian Antiquities.

doubtedly did to Greece and Rome. One argument is certainly in favour of Egypt, which is this, that the Hindoo Shaster, or Sacred Book of their law, most positively prohibits the inhabitants of India from passing the Attock, or Indus, on pain of being excommunicated: consequently it is to be inferred that the religion was brought from Egypt to India.

In the great question concerning priority of Pagan idolatry, and of its introduction, ab origine, from various countries of the east intermingling one with another, we have a curious document given by the intelligent Mr. Waddington, in his Travels in Ethiopia, who is inclined to give the preference to Ethiopia over that of Egypt, or Thebes, and has argued the position in a manner well worthy of detailing in this place.

"The question (says he) naturally presents itself—to which of these two countries the worship common to both is indebted for its origin, into which I shall only enter by comparing a few of the passages of ancient authors, that bear most upon the subject; and by a repetition of the opinions formed by me on the spot, with respect to the antiquity of the ruins already described.

"We learn from Herodotus that Sesostris was the only Egyptian who was ever master of Ethiopia. And Strabo speaks of a sacred mountain in Ethiopia, where was a temple of Isis, built by that conqueror. From this assertion, and from this only in history, it might, for a moment, be suspected that Sesostris introduced into that country the religion of Egypt. The facts that destroy such a supposition are, first, the short duration of Egyptian influence in Ethiopia, which ceased at the death of the monarch who first planted it there; and seems to have so little affected the power and energy of that kingdom, that in little more than a century afterwards, we find the armies of Memnon redeeming the honour of their fathers, and his statues erected among the temples of Egyptian Thebes. The second is drawn from Herodotus himself, who briefly mentions, that before the time of Sesostris there had been three hundred and thirty kings of Egypt, of whom eighteen were Ethiopians. The number may be incorrect, but if the proportion be true, it appears that, in the earliest ages of which any events are recorded in profane history, Egypt was occasionally under the sceptre of the monarchs of

Ethiopia, as it was afterwards, for fifty years, under that of Sabaco. On the other hand, Diodorus Siculus describes the Ethiopians as a people who had never been conquered by any foreigner; and that against them only, among men, Hercules and Bacchus had no success. It appears clear then, that, as far back as we have any light from history, Ethiopia was a mighty kingdom, and unlikely to have received its religion from a people to whom it not unfrequently gave laws.

"The age of kings and priests was preceded in Egypt, as in Greece, by those of gods and of heroes, which were, of course, represented to Herodotus, and believed by their worshippers, to be indigenous; so those introduced, at a much later period, from Egypt into Greece, after being corrected of their formality and extravagance, were claimed as original natives of the land where they were only re-born. But as the Egyptians never failed to remind the Grecians of their religious obligations to them, so does it appear from a very curious passage in Diodorus Siculus, that the Ethiopians boasted to have similar claims on the gratitude of Egypt, for they say that the Egyptians are a colony from them.

selves, and that Osiris led the colony, meaning that the soil of Egypt *is only the mud of Ethiopia;* that their customs, particularly with respect to the funerals of the kings, are alike; and that the shapes of their statues and the forms of their letters are Ethiopian, for of the two characters in use among the Egyptians, that called the vulgar is learnt by all, while the sacred character is intelligible only to the priests, who learn it in mystery from their fathers; whereas all the Ethiopians use this character. Thus, then, were hieroglyphics nothing more than the common language of Ethiopia; and, if this be true (as Diodorus seems to believe), there can be no doubt respecting the origin of the religion. At an age so distant, that even the records of Memphis did not pretend to reach it, some Ethiopian conqueror had taught his worship and consecrated his language in Egypt *."

Hence it would appear that the religion of Ethiopia was, in the first instance, given to Egypt; and if we couple this circumstance with the original introduction of the Cuthites

* Waddington's Travels in Ethiopia, p. 179, et seq.

from Chaldea into Ethiopia and Egypt after the migration of Shinar, we shall have opened a road to the prevailing idolatry over the greatest part of the habitable globe, whether it be that of the sun and moon, or the Sabian superstition in the worship of the heavenly bodies, from Babylon to Ipsambool in Ethiopia, to Thebes and Memphis in Egypt, to Greece, Italy, and India, to Scandinavia or Gothland, and to the shores of the British Isles, in the form and fashion of the ancient Druids.

In the year 1801 my late gallant friend, colonel John Ludlow of the Bengal establishment, accompanied general Baird's army on the expedition to Egypt. After reaching the Nile, he visited the temples of Luxor, Thebes, and more especially that of Tintyra or Dendera (Isis), where viewing the walls of these magnificent ruins, he perceived the Hindoo Sipahees of the army recognising their own deities, in representations of stone idols, of Vishnu, Siva, Bhavanee, and others, and actually performed *poojah*, or worship to them; and it is added, that they expressed great indignation towards the Egyptians, for not paying more respect to, what they termed, "their own gods." A fact so well attested cannot be questioned; and, from this circumstance, we may be justified in a presumption, that the Hindoo religion originated in Egypt, and we may likewise, by consequence, infer that the figures of Bood'h and Jeyne, who are anterior to the modern Hindoos, may still be found amidst the splendid ruins of Upper Egypt, and most probably in the island of Philoe, and the country beyond the cataracts of the Nile towards Ethiopia. Other travellers, and more especially the intelligent and ingenious Savary, had intimately explored the caverns of Egypt; and, after minute examination, discovered among them the figures of the Indian gods, Jaggernauth *, Ganneish, or Ganesa, and Vishnu. Of the

* At Ashdod in Syria was the temple of Dagon. The coincidence of the Philistine god Dagon with that of the Indian Jaggernauth is truly singular; since, in the fifth chapter of First Samuel, verse fourth, we find: "And when they arose early on the morrow morning, behold, Dagon was fallen upon his face to the ground before the ark of the Lord; and the head of Dagon, and both the palms of his hands, were cut off upon the threshold; only the stump of Dagon was left to him. Therefore neither the priests of Dagon, nor any that come into Dagon's house, tread on the threshold of Dagon in Ashdod unto this day." Now it is remarkable that the idol Jaggernauth, or Jaghannauth, "lord of the universe," is at the present day in a state nearly resembling that of his brother in Ashdod. The

same opinion was Mr. Chevalier, formerly governor of Chandernagore, in the service of the late king of France, the

Reverend Mr. Ward of Serampore, in his admirable History of the Religion of the Hindoos, expressly says, when speaking of Jaggernauth, "The image of this god had no legs, and only stumps of arms." He is a hideous, distorted monster, with fiery red eyes, and a distended mouth. The comparison here exhibited between these two idols, from the shores of the Mediterranean to those of India, is truly surprising. The temple of Dagon was on the coast of Syria, and that of Jaggernauth is on the sea-shore in the province of Orissa in Hindoostan.

I. The variety of instances to be met with in the holy scriptures of the nature of the gods of the surrounding idolatrous nations which encompassed the children of Israel on all sides, when compared with those of India and Egypt, will be found to assimilate in their general description and attributes; a circumstance which perhaps may, more than in any other shape, tend to demonstrate the truth of the Mosaic dispensation, and the divine ordinances thereunto appertaining. Amongst other instances to be seen in various parts of holy writ, we have, in the detail of king Solomon's conduct, the names of the pagan divinities whom that prince worshipped at the instigation of his idolatrous wives and concubines, after falling off from the worship of the living God. And hence Ashtoréth, the goddess of the Sidonians; Milcom, the abomination of the Ammonites; and Chemosh, the abomination of Moab, are, I think, without difficulty, resolved into, 1. Astarte (the Moon) of the Sidonians, the Isis of Egypt, and Parvati of India, Diana of Greece and Rome. 2. Milcom, the abomination of the Ammonites, מלכם Rex, Arab. ملك, Milcom and Molech, or Moloch (Hebrew), into Maha Deva (the great god) of the Hindoos, the terrible Siva. 3. Chemosh, כמוש into Shems (the unfortunate Louis XVI., who, during his journey overland from India to Europe, discovered the Indian deities in the

Sun, Arab. شمس) which that word implies in Chaldaic, Syriac, and Arabic, into the Hindoo Suruj, or Suryah, the Apollo of pagan mythology.

II. In fine, if Dagon be Maha Deva, he might have descended from Egypt to Ashdod on the coast of Syria, in the first instance; and, in the second, have been carried across the Attock to Hindoostan and the sea shore of Orissa. It is singular, likewise, that the fishy part of the idol Dagon is mentioned in holy writ (1 Kings, chap. xi. verses 5, 6, 7; 2 Kings); and it corroborates, in a remarkable degree, the Hindoo mythological doctrines, in the incarnation of Vishnu into a fish, for the preservation of the world at the general deluge, as do the attributes of his prototype Bood'h, who is declared to have issued from the mouth of a fish.

Dagon, the tutelary deity of Ashdod or *Azotus*, was the Derceti of the pagan world. Its name signifies a fish; and its figure is said to have been that of a man from the navel upwards, and that of a fish downwards. It is not improbable, says the learned Doctor Horne, "that this idol was commemorative of the preservation of Noah in the ark."—Horne on the Study of the Holy Scriptures.

Here, then, we have a manifest coincidence in the attributes of Dagon of Ashdod and Vishnu of the Hindoos; who is Bood'h in the eighth *outar*, from whence is derived the worship of the Boodhists of the present day.—AUTHOR.

Dr. Godwin, in his work entitled "Moses and Aaron," says, "The Hebrew doctors affirm that this idol Dagon was made from the navel downwards in form of a fish, but from the navel upwards in form of a man;" and farther, that the idol Dagon had his name from the Hebrew דג, *dag*, signifying in that language a fish; a striking corroboration of the foregoing remarks.—AUTHOR. Godwin's Moses and Aaron, p. 290, London, 1625.

caverns of Thebais, which are supposed coeval with the monarchy of Thebes *. The enterprising Mr. Belzoni, amongst other successful researches, opened a celebrated temple at Ipsambool, situate in Nubia beyond the great cataract of the Nile, which he describes as the largest and most extensive that had hitherto been discovered. More than two-thirds of this grand temple were completely buried in the sand, which, in some places, covered it to the height of fifty feet †. Its site, how-

* See Light's Travels, Maurice's Indian Antiquities, and Savary's Letters.

† The Egyptians, according to Lucian, were the first men who had any religious worship, built temples, raised altars, or instituted rites and ceremonies. They had the first knowledge of sacred things, and were the first preservers of sacred history.—Lucian's Syrian Goddess, translated by Dr. Francklin.

This might seem to confirm the idea, in which many concur, that Egypt gave her religion to India, and not India to Egypt.

Another striking instance is recorded by the very intelligent traveller (Wilson) regarding a representation of the fall of our first parents, sculptured in the magnificent temple of Ipsambool in Nubia. He says that a very exact representation of Adam and Eve in the garden of Eden is to be seen in that cave, and that the serpent climbing round the tree is especially delineated, and the whole subject of the tempting of our first parents most accurately exhibited: a very singular circumstance indeed, and, as far as I have ascertained, in the course of my own studies and researches, without parallel in any other part of the Asiatic world.—Author.

ever, says Mr. Belzoni, is easily recognised by four colossal figures in a sitting posture, each of which is about sixty feet high. The walls and pilasters were covered with hieroglyphics beautifully cut, and with groups of large figures in bas-relief, in the highest state of preservation. At the end of the sanctuary, or inner hall, were four figures in a sitting posture, cut out of the living rock. Are not these the representatives of Jeyne and Bood'h? And do they not, in a most remarkable manner, assimilate with the colossal figures, as found in the Dekhan, and various other parts of the great peninsula of India? If I were sure that the remaining costume of these figures had the woolly and frizzled hair of the Boodhaic statues, I would boldly pronounce the temple at Ipsambool to have been originally dedicated either to Bood'h or Jeyne, or perhaps to both*. It has been remarked by learned men, while arguing upon the merits of the temples in

* Since writing the above, I have been informed by the celebrated traveller and eminent scholar Dr. Wilson, that the Boodhaic figures in the temples at Ipsambool correspond entirely in their costume with those of Jeyne and Bood'h which he saw in my veranda at Bhaugulpore, October, 1822.—Author.

Egypt and Nubia, or Ethiopia *, that those of the former, discovered above ground, were small and ill constructed, when compared with those of the latter, where the excavations of the mountains and the colossal statues hewn out of the living rock are far superior to those of Lower Egypt. To which we may add, that the gigantic figure of Bood'h or Jeyne, upwards of seventy feet in height, which was visited by the illustrious Duke of Wellington, is actually chiseled out of the rock from whence it originated †. This circumstance, in my opinion, bears a very strong analogy in favour of a similarity in their modes of erecting works in sculpture, observable both in India and Egypt, and authorises us to assign those mighty works to one and the same race of people, viz. the Cuthites of Ethiopia and Egypt, and the Indo-Scythæ, who settled on the Ganges and in the peninsula of India.

I have no doubt, in my own mind, but the woolly-headed Jeyne figures of Hindoostan are of Ethiopic origin; and it is not to be looked upon as a proof of the fallacy of my opinion,

* Waddington.

† East India Gazetteer, and Bryant's Analysis.

because the modern Nubians, or Abyssinians, have not woolly hair. A lapse of ages may have changed the physical costume of the remotest inhabitants of the earth *.

MEMNON.

The far-famed statue of Memnon has excited the attention of the antiquary during a series of ages from the time of Herodotus † to the present day; and conjecture has been infinite as to the real design of this enormous mass of sculpture, which, of itself, presents a specimen of the wonders of the ancient world, and indicates the colossal magnitude of the empire in

* In a map constructed by Colonel Leake, of the Royal Artillery, is the following remark: "The ancient temples above Philoe in Ethiopia are of two different kinds: those executed in the rocks at Girgee and Ipsambul rival even the grandest works of the Egyptians."

† Asiatic Researches. Herodotus, Euterpe. Even modern travellers are all agreed in respect to the size and dimensions of this enormous statue. It is of black basalt, one hundred and sixty feet in height; and it is affirmed that a stout, thick-set man, with expanded arms, could with difficulty encompass the great toe of the statue.—AUTHOR.

which it was erected*. The luminous Faber has identified the Egyptian Memnon with the Bood'h of India: he was the ancient god of the Chasas, Chusas, or Cuthites, the idolatrous descendants of Chus, and he was the same both in title and person as Mahaman, or Bood'h, the great second father of mankind. This god was also found at Susa, the ancient Chusistan, or land of the descendants of Chus, and the whole region was called Chusa Dwyp †.

Memnon is mentioned in Virgil as having conducted a body of troops from Ethiopia to Troy, when besieged by the Greeks; and he and his followers are equally designated by the poet, as being of a dark or swarthy complexion:

"Eoasque acies, et nigri Memnonis arma ‡."

* "It appeared to me (says Belzoni, whilst contemplating the ruins at Luxor) like entering a city of giants, who, after a long conflict, were all destroyed, leaving the ruins of various temples as the only proof of their former existence." Does not this forcibly recal to the reader's contemplation the magnificent works of the giant progeny of Ham, so frequently alluded to, and which are to the present day viewed with admiration in so many parts of the eastern world?—AUTHOR.

† Faber, passim.

‡ Æneid.

The black colour, here alluded to, was in consequence of the statue of Memnon, like those of Bood'h and Jeyne in India, being of a dark coloured basalt, intending to represent Memnon as a black man, or Ethiopian; and the curled or woolly hair, discoverable in the statues of Bood'h and Jeyne, is proverbial. The Osymandes of the Egyptians is thought to be the same as Memnon, and Memnon is so much the counterpart of Sesostris, one of the most ancient of the dynasty of the Egyptian kings, that these three personages may be considered as one, and all are ultimately resolved into the elder Bood'h of Hindoostan *.

CAVERNS AT THEBES.

The grottoes or excavated chambers to be seen at Thebes in Upper Egypt constitute one of the principal curiosities of that celebrated capital, and give us a very high idea of the wealth and power of the monarch who caused them to

* Faber.

be consecrated. They consist of regularly formed double galleries of stone, supported by pillars; and, whilst traversing their dark recesses, one might be tempted to believe that they were receptacles of the dead, were we not informed by ancient historians that they served as subterraneous dwellings for the primitive inhabitants of Egypt, and were, in fact, the people called Troglodyte *, an appellation emphatically characteristic of their condition and mode of life. In proportion as the height of these galleries increases, they are seen more richly decorated, and exhibit magnificent paintings and sculpture. These † are supposed, in later times, to have been the tombs of the kings of Egypt; and the laboured and highly finished sculptures, the figures, embellishments, and devices, that are observable in every part of these wonderful excavations, sufficiently attest that they were actually the repositories of the dead. (The plan of these excavations is no less singular and interesting; some of the chambers are so complicated and

* From τρωγλη, a cave, and δυνω, to enter, or dwell in.

† Denon's Travels, English edition.

winding, that one might suppose that they were designed for a labyrinth, a species of whimsical architecture observable both in Egypt and Greece.) The intelligent French traveller, Denon, supposes that these subterranean labyrinths, and their complicated windings and passages, might probably be intended for the mysterious celebration and trials of the initiated, who became members of the Egyptian priesthood. Long and gloomy galleries, winding backward and forward, occupy a very large extent of ground: these open into other chambers, through narrow paths, and lead to deep perpendicular pits, which the traveller is compelled to descend by resting his arms against the sides, and fixing his feet in steps, cut out of the rock for the purpose. At the bottom of these pits are other chambers, and still lower a second series of pits and chambers, horizontally placed; and, finally, after traversing these gloomy abodes, the traveller ascends a lofty flight of steps, and gains a level open space, near the spot where he first entered. It is impossible not to be struck with the similarity in this description to that of Apuleius, whilst detailing the rites and ceremonies at the celebration of the mysteries of

Eleusis: from hence it is fair to conjecture that Greece received her knowledge of those mysterious rites from Egypt*. Nothing in the history of pagan mythology is more memorable or illustrious than the festival of Ceres Eleusina. The origin of the institution is referred to the goddess herself; who, coming to Eleusis, in the reign of Erectheus, and finding the country afflicted with famine, taught the inhabitants the culture of corn, and instructed them in the principles of justice and humanity. Those mysteries were divided into the greater and lesser. Those who desired to be initiated into the greater

* It is a generally received opinion among the eastern nations, that the more noble buildings of the antediluvian world were not destroyed; and that many temples, and other edifices still extant, having been originally hewn out of the solid rock, could not be injured by time, climate, or the flood of the deluge, and were most unquestionably the work of the artists of the old world. Another ingenious solution of the design of the before mentioned caves has been given by the energetic Bruce, the eminent Abyssinian traveller, who conjectures that they were designed to be Christian churches, hewn out of the solid rock, by order of Laillabala, a king of Abyssinia, A.D. 1200. Which of these two were the original intention, we leave to the judgment of our readers; but, for my own part, I lean to the first mentioned supposition.—Author. Denon, passim. Bruce's Travels, 8vo edit. vol. ii. p. 444.

mysteries were prepared and purified by watching, temperance, sacrifices, instruction, and prayer; and, previous to the initiation of the mysterious secrets, the most profound silence was enjoined them. When the time for their initiating arrived, they were brought into the temple, and, to inspire the greater reverence, the ceremony was performed in the night: wonderful things passed upon the occasion, visions were seen, and voices were heard of an extraordinary nature; a sudden splendour illuminated the darkness of the place, and, immediately disappearing, added new horrors to the gloomy apparitions; claps of thunder, the shaking of the earth, heightened the terrors and amazement, while the trembling candidate heard the mysterious volumes read to him by the hierophant *.

* Rutherford, vol. ii. Speaking of the Troglodytes, Mr. Waddington has remarked, that a people little removed from the deluge, and living in dread of its return, naturally sought the sides of mountains, and built their habitations in solid rock. He is also of opinion that the sculptured caverns in Nubia are of a higher antiquity than the columns of Thebes.—AUTHOR.

CHAPTER IV.

BOOD'H *.

THE religion of Bood'h is unquestionably more ancient than that of Brahma, and contradicts some essential points of

* The etymological derivations of this word, says the learned Dr. R. Tytler, that have been offered in the writings of various authors, are innumerable. It has been looked for in the Persian verb *Boodun*, بودن *to be*, in the English *Bode*, and Sanscrit *Veda*; *b* and *v* being letters mutually convertible into each other, together with vocables in many other tongues. But on the present occasion verbal deduction, carried to great extent, would rather obscure than illuminate. I therefore relinquish the assistance that, under other circumstances, etymology might afford, satisfying myself with remarking that, in the language commonly employed in Hindoostan, *Boodha*, or *Budha*, signifies an old or venerable man; and hence this vocable, divested of every idea, except what its vulgar meaning supplies, leads us to expect, when appropriated as the denomination of a mythological character, a sanctified *muni*, devotee, or priest, exclusively occupied in continual devotion to the Deity. But those Hindoos who reverence the worship of Bood'h contend, that he is an incarnation of Vishnu in the form of mercy, and the last grand *outar* of this member of the triad that has appeared in the world.—Tytler's Inquiry into the Theories and Principles of Budaic Sabeism, Calcutta, 1817, p. 83, 4to.

the latter, particularly concerning the creation and the immortality of the soul. It is a question, the learned Dr. Ward * has observed, that has not yet been completely decided, whether the religion of Bood'h, now spread over the Burman empire, be not in reality the most ancient religion of India; and the Brahminical superstition, at present paramount, be not the invention of later times, and raised to predominancy by the superior influence of the Brahmins with the princes of Hindoostan. Of this I myself entertain no doubt, and trust that, in the course of the present discussion, I have already produced testimonials that will be deemed satisfactory. It is certain, that among the six schools of philosophy formerly so famous among the Hindoos, two of them inculcated doctrines respecting the first cause of things that were decidedly atheistical, or such as the followers of Bood'h maintain at the present day; and it is evident, that two sects were numerous before the appearance of Bood'h. These sects were evidently the Jeynes,

* Ward on the Hindoos, 4to. edit. Calcutta. Waddington's Travels in Ethiopia.

the pure and genuine remains of the ancient Gymnosophists of India, the representatives of those naked philosophers who flourished during the invasion of India by the Greeks, whom that conqueror visited in person, and held the so much celebrated discourse, circumstantially detailed by Palladius, and other authors *.

The late Sir William Jones was of opinion, that the ruling power, on the banks of the Ganges, was, at a very remote period, the sect of Bood'h and Jeyne, since an inscription found in the neighbourhood of Baddal bore date so late as about the time of our Saviour.

From the best accounts extant, it appears that about seven hundred years before the commencement of the Christian era, *Veera Vahoo*, of the race of Goutama, or Guadma, Samona Codom, a follower of one of these sects, violently usurped the throne of Delhi. This king and his immediate successors reigned one hundred and eight years. *Maha Peti*, or lord of the universe,

* Ward on the Hindoos, vol. ii. p. 383, 4to. edit. Palladius de Gentibus Indiæ, etc.

was the third; and most writers agree in placing the era of Bood'h in the sixth century before Christ; and it is supposed that Bood'h was the son or relation of the aforementioned sovereign *.

It is admitted generally, in the opinion of the learned Dr. Ward, that he chose an ascetic life, and embraced a

* Ward on the Hindoos. Bood'h is the ninth outar; and the following legend is given of his origin. The giants applying to Indra to know by what means they could obtain the dominion of the universe, were answered, that they could only obtain it by sacrifice, purification, and piety. They made preparations for a solemn sacrifice and general ablution; but Vishnu, at the instigation of the gods, descended at the house of *Jina*, at Bood'h Gaya, in south Berar, as a Sunniasi named Bhudda, with his hair braided in a knot on the crown of his head, wrapped in a squalid mantle, with a broom in his hand. He presented himself to the giants, and was kindly received by them; but when they expressed their surprise at the foulness of his vesture, and the singular implement he carried in his hand, he told them it was cruel and impious to deprive any creature of life, and that whatever might be said in the Vedas (scriptures), every sacrifice of an animal was an abomination, and that purification was also wicked, because some small insect might be killed in washing clothes. That he never bathed, but constantly swept the ground before him, lest he should accidentally tread upon some innocent reptile; [here is the essence of the Jeyne rule of faith;] and he expatiated on the inhumanity of giving harm to animals. So eloquent was his reasoning, that the giants shed tears, and thenceforward abolished all thoughts of ablution and sacrifice.

system of philosophy already prevalent in India. The sect being thus established by *Maha Peti*, he was succeeded by eleven Boodhaic sovereigns, who reigned two hundred and ninety-one years: but their authority was at length overthrown; and *Doomundhuie*, according to Dr. Ward, after destroying the last of the Boodhaic kings, assumed the government; and from that time, about three hundred years before the Christian era, we may date the persecution already mentioned of the Boodhists.

A bloody persecution then followed upon the remainder of the devoted sect, whom the modern Brahmins wished totally

Whether Bood'h was a sage, a hero, or leader of a colony, cannot be ascertained. It is, however, certain that he was not an Indian. It might be conjectured that Bood'h, in his capacity of Guadma, or Samono Codom of the Brahmins, may be classed with the Cadmus of Greece, who was the leader of a colony, and built Thebes, and many other large cities of Greece. See Ovid's Metamorphoses. In all his images we may trace an appearance resembling that of the Egyptians and Ethiopians; and both in features and dress they differ from the acknowledged deities of the modern Hindoos. The flat nose, thick lips, and coarse, crisped, woolly hair, are permanent throughout India.—Author.

to extinguish and cut off from the face of the earth*. To avoid the malice of their enemies, therefore, the Boodhists emigrated, as we have before seen, to different countries, and gave to the respective nations those tenets and religious doctrines for which they had so sedulously contended on the plains of Hindoostan†.

The religion of the Boodhists appears to be of a singular nature. They are affirmed not to believe in a First Cause; and they consider matter as eternal: that every portion of animated existence has in itself its own use, tendency, and destiny; that the condition of creatures on earth is regulated by works of merit and demerit; that works of merit not only raise individuals to happiness, but, as they prevail, raise the world itself to prosperity: while, on the other hand, when vice is predominant, the world degenerates, till the universe itself is dissolved. Such is the strong language and doctrines of this extraordinary religion; and in it we may trace the principles of materialism in Asia to one of its primitive sources. In

* Ward, passim.

† Ibid.

the account of the Jeynes, hereafter to be detailed, we shall find nearly the same extraordinary tenets obtaining; and from both we may draw conclusions highly favourable to the truth of our own pure and holy faith.

The Boodhists, however, suppose that there is always some supreme deity, who has attained to this elevation by his superior merit; but they do not regard him as governor of the world. To the present grand period of time they assign no less than five deities; four of whom have already appeared, including Goutama, or Guadma, the Bood'h of the Brahmins, whose exaltation continues five thousand years. After the expiration of that period, another saint, or holy person, will obtain the ascendancy, and be deified. It is from the triplication of Bood'h, in his capacity of great father of mankind, that three different sects of Boodhists have emanated; namely, Bood'h or Guatama, Cadmus; Jain or Jina; Arrhan* or Mahiman. Jain and Arrhan are ultimately the same as Bood'h; just as Brahma and Vishnu of the modern Brahmins are iden-

* Faber on Pagan Idolatry.

tified with Shevan, or *Siva*, the great destroying power; and the three reigned conjointly, from that triad of great gods which was thought to be produced by the mysterious self-triplicating power of the great father. So far the learned Faber; and to this may be added the wonderful coincidence of these doctrines and the worship of Bood'h, so visibly obtaining in the remotest parts of the world, so far distant from each other, though bearing the stamp of a common antiquity, coeval with the deluge and second renovation of mankind, by divine ordination, in the person of the patriarch Noah, or the elder Bood'h *. Boötes, or Butes, in the celestial sphere, seems to be the same as Bood'h of Hindoostan; who, according to the belief of the modern Brahmins themselves, was the ninth incarnation of Vishnu; who had previously appeared in the form of a man issuing from the mouth of a fish †. He is

* Faber, passim.

† The fish represents the Ark, on which the ogdoad, or eight sacred personages, were preserved at the universal deluge. This ogdoad consisted of the diluvian patriarch Noah and his family. They were the same as Sydyk (the just) and his seven sons, the *Cabiri* (or great ones), as described by Sanchoniatho. They

represented as mild and beneficent, and adverse to bloodshed. This was doubtless an emblem of the ark, and the egress of the great patriarch and second father of mankind from that vessel, after so long a seclusion in the gloom of its recesses. It may here be remarked that, according to Sanchoniatho, the Egyptian god Taautus, or Thoth, is the same mythological character in various parts of the world; that he is the Hermes of the Greeks, the Mercury of the Latins, the Bood'h of the Hindoos, the Fo, or Fohi, of the Chinese, and the Woden of the Scandinavians; or, in other words, according to the opinion of the learned Faber, all these ancient personages are equally resolved into the patriarch Noah; that the seven *Cabiri* and the seven Titans are the family of Noah; and that Missur, or Mizraim, and the sons of the Cabiri, are the grand-children of the same illustrious ancestor, the postdiluvian patriarch: a most remarkable and singular conclusion,

are the same as the sacred ogdoad, or eight primitive gods of Egypt, who guided the ship of the sphere; thus making the ark an emblem of the celestial system.—See Faber's Cabiri, and Bryant's Analysis.—AUTHOR.

and a never-failing key in unfolding the intricate mysteries of ancient mythology.

It appears, from a translation from the *Pali*, or vernacular language of Ceylon, that about two thousand three hundred and sixty-two years ago, the religion of Bood'h in that island was pure and unmixed with any other religion whatever. About that time, however, there arose certain priests, who, going about naked, were thence called *Nigantha*, or naked men; and, contrary to the religion of Bood'h, called themselves Boodhists.

After Bood'h attained to the state called *nerwana*, or beatitude, schism began to prevail among the priests of that religion. Some of them asserted that he who had destroyed sin had no need of clothing; and, influenced by this idea, had the images of Bood'h made, cast, or painted without clothing. And thus the religion of Bood'h by small degrees began to be corrupted.

Some others of the schismatics, without covering the privities, had the image made with a loose robe thrown across the upper part of the body; and therefore there are, at this present time, four different sects of Boodhists on the continent, known by the names of *Nigantha*, *Jener*, *Jayna*, and *Samana* Boodhists.

The priests of Nigantha Bood'h go completely naked. The Jener Boodhists are worshippers of the image which is naked from the middle under, but having a loose robe across the breast.

The accompanying figure of Bood'h seems to have a loose robe across the breast; and is, therefore, not a true figure of Bood'h; nor is it a Nigantha figure of Bood'h, but expressly the figure which the Jener, Jayna, and Samana Boodhists worship; as these three sects worship precisely the same figure. And thus it is called by some the Jener Bood'h, by others the Jayna Bood'h, and by others the Samana Bood'h. The figure is the same in all respects with the true Bood'h, with the exception that the true Bood'h is clothed.

The Nigantha is naked *; and the Jener Bood'h is naked

* The foregoing account I received in a letter from my old and valued friend and school-fellow, the Reverend George Bisset, chaplain at the island of Ceylon; a gentleman whose unwearied labours in the cause of Christianity entitle him to

from the middle downward, and has a loose robe across the breast.

The Jeynes and Boodhists, it appears, worship the same image; but hold a different opinion with regard to the priesthood; and, in fact, the names of Jener, Jayna, and Samana, all apply to the worshippers of Bood'h.

If, therefore, the period when this schism is said to have occurred be admitted to be correct, the latter schismatics, or Jeynes, as most likely was the case, migrated from Ceylon, and carried their religion and doctrines along with them to the interior of Hindoostan; and must have been what are termed by Greek and Roman authors Gymnosophists, or naked philosophers, the Brachmanes of ancient India, and disciples of Dindamis, whose celebrated conversation with Alexander the Great has so frequently been quoted by the learned of all ages *.

the applause and esteem of his countrymen at home. It was translated from the *Pali* by a Boodhist priest who had been converted to Christianity; and may therefore, I should presume, be deemed authentic.—AUTHOR.

* See the fourth part of Palibothra.

A drawing of a figure of Bood'h or Jeyne was sent by me, in 1816, to my

G. Scharf lithog.

Printed by C. Hullmandel.

SEMI-COLOSSAL FIGURE OF BOOD'H.

Found near the Ruins of Jynuggur, in the District of Bhaugulpoor. A.D. 1819.

In later times, about one thousand years back, the Jeynes and Boodhists were again persecuted, and expelled from India; when they carried with them their doctrines and tenets to China and Japan.

Bood'h obtains particularly in Thibet. The principal idol in that celebrated region is *Mahimoonee*, or *Mahiman*, the great father, the Bood'h of lower India; who is worshipped under this and other titles and various epithets throughout Tartary, and amongst the countries east of the Berhampooter. He is the same object of worship in Assam, Ava, Siam, Japan, China, Bengal, and Hindoostan; in which several regions he is distinguished under the appellations of *Guadama*, or

learned friend Mr. Bisset, at Ceylon; and which, though not precisely the same as those found on that island, bore sufficient indications of a near relationship. The image, which is in my possession, was found near the fort of Jynaghur, in the vicinity of Sooruj-Ghurra. The costume of that figure is woolly-headed, thick lips, long ears, and confirms a conjecture that the woolly-headed figures found all over India had the countenances of negroes, as well as those of the ancient Etrurians: a very curious and interesting coincidence, and strongly tending to corroborate the antiquity of the Jeyne and Bood'h worship in India; as likewise to give a confutation of the assumed priority of religion among the modern followers of Brahma.

Guadma, Samana, Amida *. But Foh, Bood'h, Dhurma Rajah, and Mahamoonee, are all, in fact, resolved into the patriarch Noah, the second father of mankind. The images of Bood'h which are seen throughout these diversified and widely-extended countries appear frequently seated upon a throne placed upon elephants, or with elephants on each side, in a position rampant, sometimes encircled by the serpent Seesh Naga, and at other times in a regal habit, accompanied by attendants. In most of the modern images he is represented as sitting with his legs folded across, his right hand upon his thigh, and his left in his lap. A yellow covering, of a thin texture, is thrown over his left shoulder. His hair is generally in a curly state, like that of an African; his ears long, and distended by heavy rings.

The learned Kæmpfer, who was in Japan in the year 1690, speaking of the idols of that country, observes, that in the course of his embassy to Jedo, he twice visited the temple of Dabys, which he renders Daibood, or more properly *Deo-*

* Faber, passim

Bood'h, Bood'h the divinity, the god Bood'h. The temple of Daibood (says he) was opposite the gate, and in the middle of the court. The pillars were excessively large, and at least a fathom and a half thick: the idol was gilt all over, and of an incredible size; it was sitting after the Indian manner, cross-legged, on a *tarate*, or lotus-flower, the leaves of which stood upwards by way of ornament; and they were both raised about two fathoms and a half from the floor. The origin of this religion (continues Kæmpfer) must be looked for among the Brahmins. I have strong reason to believe, both from the affinity of the manner, and the very nature of the worship, that Kæmpfer meant the same person whom the Brahmins called *Buddha,* and believe to have been an essential part of Vishnu; and Vishnu is the preserving power *.

* Kæmpfer's Account of Japan. It may here be remarked, that as the elder Bood'h has been clearly identified with Noah, Bacchus, Mercury, and Cerberus; so, according to the excellent Faber, the triad of Shem, Ham, and Japhet, sons of Noah, like Jupiter, Neptune, and Pluto of the Greeks, and Brahma, Vishnu, and Siva of the Hindoos, when taken separately and in succession, are each the patriarch Noah, worshipped in conjunction with the sun, the essence and foundation of the Helio-arkite worship, which afterwards obtained throughout the pagan world. Faber on the Cabiri, vol. ii. 8vo. edit.

The Chinese and Japanese call him Buds and Siak, i. e. *Bood'h* and *Saca.* The people of Siam represent him under the form of a Moor, in a sitting posture, and of a prodigious size: his skin is black and his hair curled, or woolly, and the images about him are of the same complexion. Here we perceive the true Bood'h or Jeyne of Hindoostan; and it may reasonably be inferred, that at the time the schism, before mentioned, took place at Ceylon in the first instance, and the bloody persecutions of the followers of this sect in the second, both parties migrated, and carried their worship along with them to distant regions.

The Hindoos, or blacks, so named from their complexion, are supposed to be the same as those, who are termed by the learned Bryant, *Hindoo Scythian,* or *Cuthites,* the posterity of Ham, from Chus his son. They were those who migrated from the plains of Shinar, after the confusion of tongues by Divine appointment; and who, on the dispersion of the nations, came and settled on the banks of the Indus, or *Sind* river; after which, a colony of them migrated to Egypt, and settled in Ethiopia, above the cataracts. Those were all descendants of

Chus, the son of Ham, whose ancestors, according to the learned Bryant, were employed in the construction of the Tower of Babel; and, after their dispersion for that impious attempt, carried their arts and sciences along with them *. The Hindoo Scythians, therefore, are descendants of that giant progeny, the posterity of Ham, who have made themselves so conspicuous for their arts, learning, and feats of arms over various kingdoms of the earth. The wisdom of the Egyptians and Ethiopians was proverbial amongst the nations of antiquity, and was especially alluded to in the Sacred Scriptures, where Solomon is declared to have exceeded in wisdom, even the wisdom of the Egyptians †. Are not these people the origin of the modern Jeynes and Boodhists, whose large colossal statues, woolly heads, and thick lips, sufficiently indicate their Ethiopic origin ‡, observable over so great a part of the

* Bryant's Analysis.

† 1st chapter of Kings, verses 1, 2.

‡ At Ghirfeh Hussun, in Ethiopia, the celebrated traveller Leigh found an excavated temple, which exhibited a stupendous monument of the labour bestowed by the ancients on their places of devotion, and which, I have no doubt in my own mind, was Boodhaic. He says the area or outer court is formed of six columns on

eastern world, and who, in early times, extended even to Germany, and the shores of the British ocean? The works of this extraordinary race are to be seen both in Asia and Africa. At the time that the Cuthite Ethiopians arrived in Egypt, and expelled the Mizraim, or aborigines of that country, Lower Egypt was, in a great measure, a morass; but, under their descendants, says the learned Bryant, it was drained by numerous canals, and rendered the most beautiful country in the world; they carried a sluice with vast labour from the Pelusiac branch of the Nile to the western gulf of the Red Sea, part of which remains to the present day, and passes

each side, attached to which are statues of priests rudely sculptured. The area is sixty-four feet in length, and thirty-six in breadth: the width of the door into the temple is six feet, and the passage is formed by three immense columns, to which are attached colossal statues of priests; they stand on pedestals, three feet three inches high, and are themselves eighteen feet six inches in height. They are ornamented with girdles, carrying each a crosier, or cruciform hammer, in their hands; and their rich dress, formerly covered with paint and gold, and gigantic proportions, have a most imposing appearance. Here then we have the true colossal Boodhaic statue with its relative and appropriate costume, seen equally in the temples of Hindoostan and Upper Egypt, and strongly corroborative of the positions already advanced upon this interesting subject.—Author.

through Grand Cairo towards Mutineah, and account for the vastness of design, and excellenee of execution, which are so manifestly discernible in those wonderful fabrics. The pyramids, and the principal obelisks of Egypt, were erected by them. In India, the stupendous caverns of Elephanta and Salsette, the temples of Canara and Eloura in the Dekhan, and many others were, in all probability, the work of their hands; and in this we may visibly trace their Chaldaic origin, since the Cuthites* or posterity of Ham, according to the learned Bryant, who came from Babylonia, and conquered Egypt, were no other than the nation who, in after times, were called Scuthæ and Scythæ, or Scythians, and were esteemed the most ancient of any nation upon earth: they were the first

* Among the ancients there were two places called Cush, eastern and western. There was a Cush in Asia and a Cush in Africa. That the western Cush was Ethiopia all are agreed. The eastern Cush, in all probability, denotes a country beyond the Ganges, which, in description, would seem to answer for modern China; and the Chinese history has some traditions extremely analogous to the Mosaic dispensation. This circumstance, in my opinion, seems to connect the eastern and western analogies in point of religious worship, in a very remarkable manner.—AUTHOR.

after the deluge who constituted a large kingdom, and lived under a regular government. But I shall go still further, and show, from the best authority, that the religion of Bood'h and Jeyne existed in Ceylon from the most remote antiquity; the Scythæ, or Scythians of antiquity *, being no other than the descendants of Chus; and that, at a very remote period, they occupied the country on the banks of the Indus, or Sind river, which is called by the author of the Periplus, *Sinthus*, which Mr. Bryant identifies with the Indus. The author of the Periplus says that it is the largest river that runs into the Erythræan Sea, meaning the Persian Gulf, for both gulfs were denominated by the ancients *Erythræan;* that they occupied the lower and flat part of the peninsula called *Juzirat*, the Arabic word for island, the modern Cutch; and from their ancestors, as well as from their worship, they called it Cambaia, or the bay of Cham, one of the names of Chus, signifying the sun, which it retains to the present day. They afterwards, says the learned antiquarian, settled upon the promontory of

* Bryant's Analysis, pascim.

Comar, or Cape Comorin, and were lords also of the great island of Palæsemunder*, called afterwards Selan Dive, Serindib, *Selandeep, Singhala Dwypa*, or Island of lion-like men, Seilaun, and Ceylon †, in which island, as we have already seen ‡, the Boodhist rites obtain at the present day; and their large colossal figures with their thick lips, cross-legs, and woolly hair, are sufficiently indicative of their being the representatives of their great progenitor Ham: they were styled the *southern Skuthæ*, or south Scythians, of whom the poet Dionysius has given an animated description.

That this Scythia was the land of *Cutha* is evident from its being styled Ethiopia; under which character it is alluded

* *Palæsemunder.* Might not this word have formerly been two, viz. *Pali Samunder*, the sea of Pali?

† See Bryant's Analysis, vol. iv. 8vo. edition.

‡ Bryant says, in speaking of Palæsemunder or Ceylon, that in that island was a pike or peak, sacred to Adam, which was held in the highest estimation by the *Palis*, or native inhabitants of that celebrated island; but, in his opinion, it was not of antediluvian credence, with respect to the great father of mankind, but rather to his posterity in the person of Ad Ham, the king or deity Ham, the Ammon of the Egyptians.—Bryant's Analysis.

to by Eusebius. The Cuthites, moreover, worshipped Noah, under the name of Nusos and Dio-Nusos, the divine Nusos; and wherever they came they built cities to his memory, called Nusa, the *Nysæa* of Quintus Curtius, Arrian, and others. They also worshipped Chus under the character of Iacchus, or Bacchus; and their history is considered by the learned author before mentioned * to be shadowed out in their dispersion and flight from Babel, and is traditionally recorded in most places where they settled, but more especially in those of the Indian Cuthites, or Cuthite progeny of Ham, who, as we have already seen, established themselves in several parts of Hindoostan, and the neighbouring countries. To prove the priority of these descendants of Ham over the moderns, I quote the words of that learned antiquarian, who says, after stating that the Cuthites had reached Hindoostan, and there introduced their religion, and given proof of their superior attainments in arts and sciences, "that every thing in these countries, i. e. India and its adjacent islands, savours of Chal-

* Bryant, passim.

dean and Egyptian institutions: the worship of the ape (Hanuman), of the parent cow (Kamdhenu), the symbolical adoration of the serpent, Sees Naga, Vasuka, and Amunta, have been introduced by people from those parts; but not so much by the Misraim, or aborigines of Egypt, as by the Cuthites."

But to return to Bood'h: under the character of Bood'h, the learned Bryant thinks we may trace the memorials of the ark *, and of the persons preserved in it. Kæmpfer, in speaking of the emperors of Japan †, observes that, in the reign of *Syu Mu*, the Boodhist rites commenced in that island; and adds, that *Budo*, or *Bood'h*, otherwise called *Kobotus*, came over from the Indies into Japan upon a white horse, and brought with him his religion and doctrines. Here, says Bryant, the object of the worship is made the person who introduced it. In this short account what a history is unfolded ‡! Indeed, it is a most curious circumstance, and clearly proves the antiquity of the worship of Jeyne and Bood'h, who are

* Bryant's Analysis.

† Kæmpfer's Japan.

‡ Ward on the Hindoos, vol. ii. Calcutta 4to. edition.

known to be identified with each other in the last *outar* of the modern Hindoos. I think the white horse is especially mentioned as to appear at the end of time; and the notice taken of Death on the pale horse * at the consummation of all things, as related in the Sacred Scriptures, would appear to bear a strong affinity.

The Boodhists do not believe in a first cause: they consider matter as eternal; that every portion of animated existence has in itself its own ruin, tendency, and destiny; that the condition of creatures on earth is weighed by works of merit and demerit; that works of merit not only raise individuals to happiness, but as they prevail, raise the world itself to prosperity; while, on the other hand, when vice predominates, the world degenerates till the universe is dissolved †.

* Revelation of St. John.

† "The religion of Bood'h (says Captain Mahoney) as far as I have had any insight into it, seems to be founded in a mild and simple morality. Bood'h has taken for his principles, wisdom, justice, and benevolence; from which principles emanate ten commandments, held by his followers as the true and only rule of their conduct."

They suppose, however, that there is always some superior being, who has attained to this elevation by religious merit; but they do not regard him as governor of the universe; though the word *Tirtunkar* certainly implies "supreme director of affairs." Hence the doctrine would appear incongruous.

The lowest state of existence among the Boodhists is in hell; the next is that in the form of brutes: both of these are in a state of punishment for demerit. The next ascent is to that of man, which is probationary. The next includes various degrees of honour and happiness, which carries them up to demi-gods, or rather deified mortals; which is assumed as a reward for works of merit. Lastly, The ascent to divinity is from the state of man. We see here then, in this whimsical system of the Boodhists, an evident resemblance to the metempsychosis of Ovid, and the doctrine of Pythagoras, who expressly states that he formerly inhabited the body of Euphorbus the son of Pantheus, who was slain in the Trojan war by the Grecian prince Menelaus. Pythagoras introduced this doctrine from Egypt into Greece; and is thus made by Ovid to unfold in impassioned strains the mysterious doctrine of the metempsychosis *, and to describe the transmigration of the souls of mortals after death into the bodies of animals, and vice versâ, according to their behaviour and occupations during their former state of existence; and he concludes with the very essence of the various Hindoo doctrines on this subject, whether of Brahma or of Bood'h, of Vishnu or of Jeyne.

"O genus attonitum gelidæ formidine mortis,
Quid Stygà, quid tenebras, quid nomina vana timetis,
Materiem vatum, falsique piacula mundi?
Corpora sive rogus flammâ, seu tabe vetustas
Abstulerit, mala posse pati non ulla putetis.
Morte carent animæ: semperque, priore relictâ
Sede, novis habitant domibus vivuntque receptæ.

---

* "In Troy's proud fields I bore the warlike form
Of Pantheus' son, slain by the valiant hand
Of Menelaus king."

Ipse ego (nam memini) Trojani tempore belli
Panthoïdes Euphorbus eram: cui pectore quondam
Sedit in adverso gravis hasta minoris Atridæ.

OVID. Met.

Omnia mutantur: nihil interit. Errat, et illinc
Huc venit, hinc illuc, et quoslibet occupat artus
Spiritus: *èque feris humana in corpora transit,*
*Inque feras noster: nec tempore deperit ullo**."

The Boodhists are taught that there are four superior heavens, which are not destroyed at the end of a *Kalpa*, or given period of time; that the highest state of glory is absorption into the divine essence; and yet, strange to say, they deny the existence of a separate supreme spirit: for the term *Nirvana* implies, according to the Birman derivative, only exemption from the miseries incident to humanity, but by no means annihilation. How, then, are we to account for this strange contradiction in the most essential part of their faith? It is difficult to conceive what they mean by the term "absorption into the divinity," if they do not believe in a supreme being. A Jeyne (who differs little from a Boodhist) was once asked by the learned author of the "Religion of the Hindoos," why, since the object of their worship was neither creation nor preservation, they honoured him as God? He replied,

* Ovid. Met. lib. xv. line 153, et seq.

that it was an act of homage to exalted merit. Persons among the Boodhists who perform works of exalted merit are admitted to the heavens of the different deities, or are made kings on earth; whilst those who are wicked are born in the forms of different animals, or consigned to different places of punishment. But the happiness of the heavens here described is wholly sensual, and consequently ridiculous. Five express commands are imposed upon the followers of Bood'h. The first forbids the destruction of animal life, which is precisely the case in the Jeyne doctrine. The second forbids theft; the third, adultery; the fourth, falsehood; the fifth, the use of spiritous liquors. Among works of the highest merit, they stupidly consider the feeding of a hungry infirm tiger with their own flesh to be the first.

Respecting the Hindoo deities, the Boodhists believe that Brimha or Brahma is the head of the Bramhacharies, and lives with them in one of the higher heavens; that Vishnu, Siva, Kartick, and Somina are the chief ministers of Indra, god of the firmament: and most authors are agreed that the followers of Bood'h in general hold the modern Hindoos in a lower degree of estimation than even the Mahomedans, or members of any other faith.

It appears, from the writings of the Burma Boodhists*, that the ancient religion of that empire consisted principally in religious austerities. When a person first adopted the order of the priesthood, he immediately renounced the secular state, lived on alms, and abstained from food after the sun had passed the meridian; a custom which obtains among the modern Jeynes at the present day, as I shall hereafter have occasion to notice. Among the ancient records of the Brahmins an order of female priests is likewise mentioned; but it is probable that they were only female mendicants, as great numbers of this class of persons are seen throughout Hindoostan, the region of Tibet, Tartary, and China. A priest is forbidden by law to marry. They are to live solely on the bounty of their religious countrymen; and their stock of clothes and utensils is confined to only three garments: a begging dish, to solicit alms; a girdle; a razor; a needle; and a cloth to strain the

* Ward on the Hindoos.

water which they drink, lest they should improvidently deprive an insect of life.

The priests superintend the education of youth, and they teach gratuitously as a work of merit, their pupils being maintained at home by their respective parents. Should a priest perceive that his pupil is acute, and possesses good parts, he persuades the parents to allow of the youth being destined for the order; but should the youth, of his own accord, prefer a secular life, no restraint is ever imposed on his inclinations. The initiation of a youth into these schools is impressive. The parents usually give a feast, which continues for three or four days; at the termination of which the youth, arrayed in splendid garments and ornaments, and attended by a numerous retinue, is led through the town on horseback to the college of his preceptor, or Gooroo. As soon as he arrives, he is stripped of his splendid attire; his head is shaved; he is clothed in a yellow garment, the favourite colour of the Boodhists; and a beggar's dish of wood is put into his hand. In this manner he is committed to the care of his tutor, to commence his career of study. During his tuition, he is instructed rigidly to observe the following rules of conduct: He is to abstain from the commission of murder, theft, evil desires, ardent spirits, food after the meridian, dancing, music, from flowers and perfumes, the luxurious accommodations of life, and the use of gold and silver. Should he fail in the performance of these self-denying propositions, he is disqualified from further advancement: but if he keep the rules of the obedient disciple, at the end of the prescribed period of twenty years he is admitted into the order of the priesthood *.

The injunction of precepts is carried among the Birman Boodhists still farther. Two hundred and twenty-seven other precepts are administered, the observance of which, for a period of ten years, entitles aspirants to the rank of priest of the first order, or *antistes*, and empowers him to found colleges, and have disciples of his own. Such are the means by which a Birman priest obtains a preeminence over his less persevering countrymen: and a philosopher, whilst contemplating the comparatively insignificant rules of discipline observed in the

* Ward, passim.

colleges of Europe, might either praise or deplore the *Pythagorean* strictness of a Burman university. The Boodhaic priests worship daily in the temples. The worship is. simple and chaste. It consists, like that of the Jeynes, in presenting flowers, incense, rice, betel-nut, and fruits. The priests, previous to service, carefully sweep the pavement of the temple; preserve the lights by keeping up and refreshing *the fire*; and receive the offerings. No blood is ever seen to flow on the pavement of a Boodhaic or Jeyne place of worship. The five great commandments before alluded to are solemnly repeated twice every day by the priest to the worshippers, who stand up, and respectfully repeat them after him.

A festival always precedes the opening of a temple, as at laying the foundation, and setting up the image, at the fixing of the umbrella, at the purification of the temple, and at the consecration; ceremonies which, in fact, bear a strong analogy to some observable in the Jewish ritual.

These feasts are sometimes prolonged to four or five days, when musicians and dancing-girls, the never-varying accompaniment to the ceremonials of pagan idolatry, are introduced, and various pantomimic representations are exhibited to the people *.

Adjoining to the Boodhaic temples are generally to be met with Dhuram Saleh's, or caravanserais for the benefit of strangers and pilgrims, in which are set up images of Bood'h, the never-failing umbrella, the emblem of royalty, and stone pots or begging dishes, in imitation of those used by Gotama, or Guadma, the Somona Cuddum of Ava and Ceylon and China, and the *Cadmus* of the Greeks. According to the doctrines of Bood'h, there is no distinction of caste. Polygamy is not forbidden, and it is therefore common to see a man with a plurality of wives. The Burmans are accustomed to burn their dead with many ceremonies, especially the bodies of the priests. If departing from the Burman empire we ascend to the mountainous regions of Tibet and Bootan, we still find the Boodhaic religion to be paramount in the countries from Assam to Lassa, and in the person of the regenerated Grand Lama of Trashoolombo recognise the mysterious doc-

* Ward, passim.

trines of the incarnate Bood'h. The principal idol in the temples * of Tibet is Mahmoonee, the Bood'h of India; who is worshipped, under this and various other epithets, throughout the great extent of Tartary, and amongst all the nations east of the Berhampootur. In the wide extended space over which this faith prevails, the same object of veneration is acknowledged under different titles †. Exclusive of his appellations in Assam, Ava, and Siam, in China, Hindoostan, and Tibet, he is called by the Brahmins of Tibet the Dhurma Rajah, from whence evidently springs the appellation *Jeyne Dhurmean*, or the Jeyne followers of Durma Rajah; and it is moreover affirmed, that the enormous hemispherical figure, seen in the latter country, was a type of Dhurma Rajah, or in other words an emblem of eternity.

The ritual, or ceremonial worship of Tibet, appears to differ materially from that of the modern Brahmins of India; and from many of their prejudices, such especially

* Turner's Embassy to Thibet.

† Hamilton's East India Register, 8vo. edition, London, 1815.

as relate to the perplexing distinction of castes, and the observance of innumerable idle ceremonies, as practised in Bengal at the present day,—from these the Tibetians are entirely exempt. Their religion is systematic and in order. The sovereign Lama, immaculate, immortal, omnipresent, is placed on the summit of the fabric; whilst the Hindoos, on the contrary, are perplexed by a multitude of deities.

This Lama is esteemed the vicegerent of the only one God, the mediator between mortals and the deity. He is moreover the centre of a civil government, which derives from his authority all its influence and power; he is, in fact, priest, king, and legislator, and, in this triple capacity, rules over a vast extent of country, and maintains both a spiritual and temporal interest among the remotest nations of the earth.

It appears, according to the most received testimonials, that there are four great Bood'hs, symbolically called the mouths of Brahma *, and a fifth, who is the sage or wise man. They all of them agree in one point of time with personages recorded

* Chronology of the Hindoos.

in holy writ, and their respective titles and attributes are as follows, viz.

First Bood'h *, the self-existing *Swayam Bhuva*, whose *outar* or period of time commenced 4002 years before Christ, or, according to the fictitious calculation of the Hindoos, 3,891,102; he ended his mortal career when the three first ages were complete, or, agreeably to Hindoo computation, during the commencement of the fourth age, which is fixed by the Hindoos themselves the year before Christ 3102, which agrees with Adam, the first father of mankind.

Second Bood'h, the son of Mayah, or *Illusion*, whose *outar* † or period commenced in the fictitious year of the Lotus creation 2,674,080, answering to the year before Christ 3383; and who having in vain endeavoured to correct men from their impiety, ascended to heaven, when the first period of time has

* Key to Chronology of the Hindoos.

† Faber supposes the mysterious birth of Merlin, our British enchanter, to be a transcript of the virgin birth of Bood'h, and terms him a Druidical hierophant; a singular circumstance, and, in my opinion, closely connected with the Boodhaic superstition of Asia.—Faber, vol. iii. page 323.

completely ended, being 1000 years of 360 days, answering to A. M. 984. This was clearly Enoch, the son of Jared.

Third Bood'h, the son of *Jina*, who was born for the confusion of demons or idolaters. His *outar* or period commenced in the beginning of the Cali yog, the first century of the second period of time, or second thousandth year of the world. He was seen at Magadha (south Behar) 246 years after the great deluge, or year before Christ 2100. Stated by Sir W. Jones at 3888 years before A. D. 1788. The prince, saved in the ark, becomes Noah, the son of Lamech, the second father of mankind.

Fourth Bood'h, the son of Devica, whose *outar* or period began in the 1527th year of the Cali yog or age, answering to the year before Christ 1575, and who died in the year that the sun stood still for twelve hours, e. g.* after the death of Crishna

* In the Mahabarat, Crishna, who corresponds with Bood'h, is always represented of a dark blue or black colour, as are the figures of Bood'h and Jeyne. He is the shepherd-god of the Hindoos, or Apollo Nomius of the Romans, a symbol of the sun. The twelve signs of the zodiac are the Nymphs of Harmony, and Crishna's inconstancy in roving from one to another, plainly indicates the sun's passage through the celestial bodies.—Author.

(Bood'h, the son of Devica), the sun stood still to hear the pious ejaculations of Arjoon, as he journeyed towards Bindrabund. This is the great leader and lawgiver of the Jews, Moses.

Fifth Bood'h, the sage or wise man. The one recorded in the lunar dynasty, or princes of the moon, and Bood'h the sun. He is recorded as the first prince of that race, as a ruler in that country where the first created resided. He is said to have married *Ila*, a daughter of the first Menu, from whom the lunar dynasties proceeded, and is undoubtedly Enoch, the son of Cain. Such is the reasoning of the luminous author of "A Key to the Chronology of the Hindoos *;" and from hence we may surmise in how remarkable a manner the legends of the Hindoos concur with the Holy Scriptures; and who is there that, on reflecting on this exposition, does not behold the most striking and positive proofs of the truth and excellence of Christianity?

* See the Key to the Chronology of the Hindoos, vol. ii. 8vo. edition, Cambridge, 1820.

For Enoch, the son of Jared, who was translated to heaven, is evidently a type of our Blessed Redeemer; and Bood'h, being identified with Enoch, how forcibly must an appeal to the Hindoos prove with regard to their conversion, if they were properly made acquainted with this singular coincidence of characters; and the will of Providence be thus ultimately manifested in the enlightenment of the benighted pagan world! Bood'h is termed by his followers Sacyah*, Xaca, or *Xaca*

* In the Sanscrit language Saka means an era, and is applied to the founder of an era; and in the Chronology of the Hindoo princes of India, Saka is a name or title, which has so often been assumed, that it is difficult to say to whom it is most appropriately due. According to Sir William Jones, Saka is a name of Budha. In the chronology of the kings of Magadha, by Major Wilford, the Hindoos are stated to have divided the Kali yuga into six unequal portions, or subordinate periods, called *Sakas*, because they derived their origin from six Sakas, or *mighty and glorious monarchs*, of whom three have already made their appearance, and three are still expected. The third Saka was *Salivahana* [*Salivahana* implies cross-born in Sanscrit], who is believed to have lived at the same time with our Saviour, and is represented to have corresponded with him in some of the principal features of his life. The era which bears his name commenced from his death, (namely, seventy-eight years after the Christian era), and is doubtless that adopted by the Javans, which corresponds with it within about three years; and the slight difference between them may be accounted for by the introduction of the Mahomedan mode of reckoning during the last three centuries.

Munie, commonly Shak Munie *; and they affirm that four thousand years ago, he was only an earthly sovereign in India, but, on account of his virtues and holy life, *God took him up to heaven alive*. He is moreover called *Narrayana*, an appellation of Vishnu, or the spirit of God moving on the waters.

The following table of the principal Hindoo deities will be found to correspond pretty generally with those of Greece, Rome, and Egypt; and may serve in some measure to identify a general system of pagan mythology, and to draw the respective superstitions into one focus. Many of the ceremonies in each system undoubtedly bear a striking analogy and resemblance to each other, and they have in continuation pervaded the greatest part of the eastern world; and the worship of Isis and Osiris, more especially, is nearly related in its most essential points to the depraved worship of Siva and his lascivious consort, Bhavani, or Parvati of the Hindoos.

* According to the Japanese historians [Kæmpfer's Japan] Saka lived a thousand years before our Saviour; and the worship of that country is still denominated by them the religion of Sak, or Saka.—Raffles's History of Java, vol. ii. 4to. page 68, London, 1817.

TABLE OF DEITIES.

INDIAN.	GREEK AND ROMAN.	EGYPTIAN.
Sooruj, or Suryah	Apollo	Horus
Cuvera	Plutus	
Cartikea	Mars	Papremis
Bhavani and Parvati	Juno, Minerva	Isis
Doorgah	Damater	Isis
Lacshmi	Venus	Isis
Pracriti (Bhagoati)	Venus Urania	Isis
Nareda	Mercury	Thoth
Cali	Proserpine, Hecate, Diana	Isis
Visva Karma	Vulcan	Thoth, or Hermes Trismegistus
Lacshmi II.	Ceres	Isis
Crishna	Pan and Apollo	Osiris
Ganesa	Janus	
Menu	Minos	Menes
Siva	Jupiter	Osiris and Typhon
Yama	Pluto	Serapis
Nunda	Minotaur	Apis
Vishnu	Jupiter	Horus, god of light, restorer of the universe

TABLE—continued.

INDIAN.	GREEK AND ROMAN.	EGYPTIAN.
Gunga	Styx	The Nile
Brahma	Jupiter	Osiris
Bood'h	Neptune	Osiris
Anna Purna	Ceres (Lacshmi)	Isis
Indra I.	Jupiter Tonans	Osiris
Indra II.	Jupiter Pluvius	Osiris:

With numerous others, which do not at present occur to my recollection. It may here be remarked, that the great event of the deluge, which forms so prominent a feature in our holy writ, and is, in fact, the groundwork of our Christian faith, is shadowed out in pagan mythology; first, by the death of *Adonis* of the Greeks; second, that of *Osiris* of the Egyptians; and, third, the egress from the ark of the great *fish-god* Bood'h of the Hindoos.—Author.

The Bood'h of Ceylon, though differing in some minor points from the Bood'h of India, is essentially the same. His form, dress, and attributes, generally correspond. The term Bood'h, or Boodhoo, is by the Singalese derived from the Pali, and implies *wisdom;* whilst Jeyne, or Jina, in Sanscrit *, means, *exemption from sin,* or, as given by some, *victorious over sin:* a very striking analogy, and sufficiently indicative of a common origin of the two religions. The number of Bood'hs, or deified saints in Ceylon, amount to five. Of these the Singalese believe four to have appeared already, and the fifth, who is to come, is termed *Nitree Bood'h.* The fourth or last Bood'h that appeared was Goutama, or Guadma, the Somono Cuddum of many nations, who, in the opinions of all strictly religious Boodhists, is the sole object of veneration, and, amongst the common people, the principal object of their ardent worship. Goutama Bood'h, according to their religious

* The Pali, or vernacular language of Ceylon, has a high claim to the attention of the literary world. It has long been a contested point whether the Pali or Sanscrit be the most ancient language of India. Certain it is that the Pali was the popular dialect of the country of Bood'h, *Magudha*, or South Behar, before the Boodhists were expelled from India: an event prior to the Christian era.

It is copious, and its literature contains the essence of the Boodhaic scriptures, and all the learning of Ceylon, as well as of those countries beyond the Ganges; and the Pali for many centuries has been what Sanscrit now is in India, and Latin in Europe.—Friend of India.

tracts, is supposed to have been born many times, and to have experienced several states of existence. In short, his history is the essence of the metempsychosis, and the doctrine of Pythagoras. In the fanciful mythology of the Singalese, the Bood'h of Ceylon was conceived in the womb of the queen Sododan, the sovereign of that kingdom. His birth was miraculous *. The queen, towards the end of a long journey, felt a wish to pluck a bunch of flowers in one of the royal gardens: the branch on which it grew bent down of itself to be gathered; and at one and the same instant she obtained the flower and was delivered of a son. At its birth the wonderful child walked straight forward several steps, and was surrounded at the same moment with the celestial beings. In the end, after a variety of wonderful adventures, this royal prince, divesting himself of his ornaments and emblems of sovereignty, became *Boodhoo*, or an anchoret; and after the performance of *tapasya*, or internal mental devotion, received *moksha*, or supreme felicity, and was absolved with God.

* Davy's Account of Ceylon.

This legend will be found to bear considerable resemblance to the one already described; and in it we may trace the resemblance to all the different legends that treat of Bood'h, or Jeyne, in the varied commentaries on either superstition *.

One of the chief seats of Boodhaic worship in the East is the celebrated mountain in the island of Ceylon, named Adam's Peak, though misnamed so; for the impression of the foot to be seen at the summit is evidently that of Bood'h, and has been acknowledged as such by his followers for a period of thirty centuries. This famous peak, termed by the natives *Samanella*, from Somono-Cuddum, one of the appellations of Bood'h, is situated sixty-six miles to the north-east of Columbo. The approach to it, according to the account given by the ingenious and spirited Dr. Davy, is through a variety of rich and splendid scenery, over a well cultivated country, containing many populous villages. The party reached Ratunpore, a military post about forty-three miles from Columbo, in two days, and

* Davy's Travels in Ceylon, London, 1821.

proceeding from thence to the Peak, after crossing several torrents, and one river, the Selagongo, which is a branch of the Cali Gonga, they ascended and descended alternately until they reached the foot of the Peak. The latter part of the ascent was difficult and perilous in the extreme. "The last stage of the way," says Dr. Davy, "is the most difficult of all, and the only part attended with danger. Near the summit the ascent is so precipitous, that were it not for iron chains fixed to the rocks, small would be the number of those who would complete their pilgrimage. Even with the help of these chains, accidents occasionally occur, and lives are lost." The summit of the peak is of a conical form, rising rapidly and majestically to a point. The area of the summit is, according to the computation of Lieutenant Malcolm, the intrepid adventurer who first ascended the peak, seventy-four feet in length, and twenty-four in breadth. On the apex of the rock is the object of worship, the *Sree Padum*, or sacred foot of Bood'h *, imprinted, according to tradition, by that patriarch,

* Like the Paduka near Bhaugulpore.

on his visit to the island. "It is," says Dr. Davy, "a superficial hollow, five feet three inches and three quarters in length, and from two feet seven to two feet five inches in breadth, ornamented with a margin of brass, and studded with a few gems of little value. The roof of a small temple which is built over it is lined with coloured cloths, and the margin is decorated with flowers and streamers, which give it a gay appearance *.

As a conclusive remark on the religion of Bood'h, I shall observe, that there are races of men in Asia who go by the common name of Tartars, but who are quite distinct from one another. The Huns, or proper Tartars, with their tribes of Teluts, Kirghisians, &c. form the first family; the Mandshurs, or Tunguses, form the second; and the Moguls, with their tribes of Calmucs, Buriats, &c. form the third.

These families or nations of Tartars have spread themselves in various quarters; and are intermingled, particularly

* According to the measurement of a very able observer, Lieutenant Colonel Williamson, the height of this celebrated peak is calculated not to exceed seven thousand feet from the level of the sea.

in the northern part of Asia, with other aboriginal families, as the *Teechucks*, the *Yukagirs*, the *Samoieds*, and the *Kamchadales*, *Monguls*, and *Mandshurs*. They not only prevail in Asiatic Russia, but occupy, as an independent people, the whole country bordering on it to the south.

They acknowledge, indeed, the supremacy of China, and consider themselves as under its protection; having, in fact, a family connexion with that empire; as it was one of the southern tribes of the Mandshurs, ruled by a khan, that con-conquered China in the seventeenth century, and whose descendants still govern there.

These three families of Tartars have distinct languages. In the other aboriginal families of Asiatic Russia there are four other distinct languages; and, in addition to these seven tongues, there are many dialects and intermixtures. The creed of the Greek church, which is the established religion of the Russian empire, has made but little progress in Asiatic Russia. Many of the Tartar tribes in the south-west are Mahomedans. Others of them, with the great body of the other Tartars throughout Asia, whether Huns, Monguls, or Mandshurs, are pagans.

Their system has been denominated Boodhism, or the religion of Bood'h, in contradistinction to Brahmanism. A more finished and elaborate system is usually posterior to that which is less so: but Boodhism is in many respects crude and simple, and unformed; whilst Brahmanism is the very reverse. The presumption, therefore, is that the latter is only a more finished exhibition of the former; and consequently that Boodhism is more ancient than Brahmanism. By the destruction of idolatry throughout Europe and the west of Asia, Boodhism reigns at present over a larger portion of the globe than Brahminism. Brahminism is confined to India, while Boodhism not only shares that country with it, but prevails from the very north of Tartary to the island of Ceylon, and from the Indus to Siam, China, and Japan. Its principal seat is Thibet, Bootan, and Cashgar, where a branch of the warlike *Cuthim* migrated from the plains of Shinar to the lofty regions of the Indian Caucasus. They brought with them that Boodhaic superstition which was so immediately founded on the history of paradise and the deluge; and to that peculiar form of old mythology their house seems to have pertinaciously adhered in all its other settlements, until it relinquished it either for the light of Christianity or for the imposture of Mahomed. Boodhism shows itself in various forms, and under different names. It is known very widely in Asia, under the appellation of Shamanism; the visible head of which religion, the *Dalai Lama*, resides in a magnificent palace, called Putala, or the Holy Mountain, near Lassa, the capital of the extensive region of Thibet. He is believed to be animated by a divine spirit, and is regarded as the vicegerent of the Deity on earth, and by some as the Deity incarnate. Death in the Grand Lama is nothing more, it is pretended, than the transmigration of the spirit into another body; and the Lamas, or priests, like those of Egypt respecting their bull-god Apis *, profess to be able, by certain sacred tokens, to detect the transmigrated Grand Lama in the body of a child; who, however, invariably belongs to their own order.

The authority of the Grand Lama is recognised not only

* Herodotus, Clio.

in China and Japan, but over almost the whole of the immense regions of Tartary and Thibet. Lassa, the capital, is in consequence crowded with royal and noble personages from all parts of Asia, who come to pay their homage, and to offer splendid presents to this earthly divinity *. It would appear, then, that the line of connexion with regard to pagan mythology and idolatry will run thus: Chaldea, Egypt, Greece, Rome, Germany, Gaul, and Britain. From Egypt into India, Tibet, Bootan, Tartary; to Ava, Siam, Ceylon, and the isles of the Eastern Archipelago; to Japan and China, and from thence to Siberia, Russia, Scandinavia, and the northern extremities of Europe.

The following curious answer to the celebrated traveller Bernier, from some learned Pundits at Benares, when charged by him with idolatry in their worship, will show that, under

* For the above remarks I am indebted to the valuable publication denominated "The Friend of India;" a work printed quarterly in Calcutta; whose able conductors, Drs. Marshman, Carey, and Ward have already rendered such eminent services to the cause of true religion and science, during their long residence in India.—AUTHOR.

all the circumstances of the case, they may be considered rather as unitarians than followers of polytheism. "We have, indeed," said they, "in our temples store of diverse statues, as those of Brahma, Mahadeo, Ganneish, and Bhowanni, who are some of the chief and most perfect Dewtahs; and we have also many others, of less perfection, to whom we pay great honour; prostrating ourselves to the ground before them; presenting them flowers, rice, fruits, scented oils, saffron, and such other things, with much ceremony: but we do not believe these statues to be Brahma, or Vishnu, &c. themselves, but only their images and representatives; and we do not give them that honour but upon account of what they represent. They are in our temples, because it is necessary, for praying well, to have something before our eyes that may fix the mind. For the rest, we acknowledge one only supreme lord and master, the great Creator of the universe *."

* Bernier's Travels, folio edition.

CHAPTER V.

JEYNE.

Of the modern Jeynes, or Jains, I have yet to speak. The Jeynes, properly speaking, are divided into two classes, denominated *Situmber* and *Digumber*. The former adorn their statues with garments, and with chaplets of flowers, while the latter exhibit the figures unornamented, and in a simple state of nudity, like Adam before the fall; the chief principle of both is the preservation of life, even to the minutest insect, and they eat no animal food of any kind. The Digumber is now the prevailing sect throughout Hindoostan, so that one seldom meets with any of the other class, of which *Jugut Seet*, an eminent banker of Moorshedabad, seems to have been the principal; but he has, of late years, declined, in the estimation of his own caste, from his having gone over to the principles and practice of the modern Brahmins. The Situmber appears to have prevailed principally at Bood'h Gayah, in Bengal; and accordingly all the statues there are highly ornamented, while those from Orissa and the southern provinces of the Dekhan are all naked, and standing with their hands hanging down the sides *, and are, of course, Digumber. The sect of Bood'h, which I have already shown to be identified with Jeyne, equally refrain from the destruction of animal life, but receive and eat animal food when presented to them by others, saying, that that which has no sensation may be freely eaten; a singular difference and seemingly contradictory, or at least a strange falling off from the original purity of their ancient worship.

In like manner we find the Egyptians, whose worship the learned Faber identifies with that of the elder Bood'h, were careful of the lives of animals; though we learn from Herodotus, that the priests had a daily portion of beef, geese, and swine's flesh, and wine: from which we must infer that the animals were rendered sacred and lawful to be eaten, by being

* As represented in a drawing of General Stuart's collection.

first sacrificed on the altars of the gods. It is thus also with the modern Hindoos of the *Sacti*, or Siva sect, who offer kids and buffaloes in sacrifice to Cali, at the Ghaut of that goddess near Calcutta, and in many other places throughout India; and, on such occasions, it seems indispensable that they should at least taste the meat, being thus considered as partaking of the repast with the gods.

This, however, is entirely modern; for it is evident from the *Calica Pooran*, translated by the learned Blacquire, that human victims were formerly immolated at the altars of that blood-stained goddess *.

The Jeynes do not admit that the world exists by the power of a Supreme Being; since they argue that the world is eternal and consists of matter; that its changes are natural; that it is not wholly liable to destruction, since all things are born by the power of nature; they only, therefore, believe in what is perceptible to their own organs of sense, and for this singular reason, they do not acknowledge a God

* Asiatic Researches.

in the heavens above, "because no one ever saw him," and they deem it impossible for any one to see him; but they believe in a *Tirtunkar*, or supreme director of affairs, in the person of their first prophet, or Gooroo (spiritual teacher), who attained the state of Nirvana (beatitude) by his extraordinary perfections, to the satisfaction of mankind for all ages. From time immemorial, they affirm, that they possessed the images of several successive Gooroos of their first prophet, and whose number amounts to twenty-four incarnations. These images are naked, and are worshipped in their temples as gods, rather than representatives of God. In speaking of God as their Tirtunkar *, they say he has a likeness and no likeness; they compare him to an image of transparent crystal. He is supposed to possess eight good qualities, and is exempt from the like number of evil ones. He is all-wise, all-seeing, the father or origin of all, enjoying eternal bliss,

* The adoration which the Jeynes offer up to their Tirtunkar, or deified saint, naturally refer to the Supreme Being alone, for those holy personages (says the Abbé Dubois) receiving Moksha, or supreme bliss after death, become united to the Deity.—See Abbé Dubois.

without name, without being, and without end infinite, indescribable. The eight evil qualities are ignorance, mental blindness, pain incident to nature, the distinction of name, of tribe, delusion (Maya,) mortality, illusion, immortality, dependence. He who possesses the good qualities, and has overcome the evil ones, or is superior to them, becomes god of the Jeynes, or *Jeyne Ishura,* having become incarnate in the form of their Gooroos, or Tirtunkars. This man-god, therefore, becomes the object of the worship of the Jeynes, and is considered as the sole means of his followers, through him, obtaining happiness *: such is the wild fantastic system of Jeyne worship. The Vedas of the eighteenth Puranas of the modern Brahminical system are rejected as heretical by the Jeynes; they admit, however, that these books were composed by a holy person, named Vayasa, or Beias, whom the other Brahmins acknowledge as an incarnation of the divinity.

The learned Mr. Erskine of Bombay has remarked that

* Jeyne, or Jin, implies in Sanscrit, "Victorious over Sin." Dr. F. Buchanan.

the Jeynes bear a very great resemblance to the Boodhists in their religious doctrines: they believe that there is a God, and affirm that he can be known only by such as become absorbed in his essence; that, therefore, a person knowing God ceases to possess identity; that hence it is absurd for a human being to pretend to know him; the moment you discover him, your identity ceases. They deny that God was ever incarnated; and, like the Boodhists, believe that men, by their virtuous conduct, become omniscient, and may thus be considered as infallible. They hold that, since the beginning of time, only twenty-four such superior beings have appeared for the reformation of mankind; these they style the Tirtunkar. Their priests, the Jatis, not only never put any thing to death, but never eat any thing which has had life. The Jeynes resemble the Hindoos in having castes, which the Boodhists have not. In the Mysore and the south of India, the Jeynes admit also certain of the Hindoo deities into the courts of their temples, which is never done, as far as I can learn, either in Bombay, the Mahratta country, Guzerat, or Marwar, in all of which places there are numbers of Jeynes.

In all the Jeyne temples, therefore, such images as are peculiar to the Jeyne worship are human, and distinguished only by symbols. The whole twenty-four holy saints are usually represented in one piece; and no worship is paid to their relics, nor are they placed under pyramids. There are, however, many sects of Jeynes, some professing to adhere strictly to the doctrines of one saint of the Tirtunkar, others to those of another *.

The sacred book, or scripture of the Jeynes, is called Yogue (path or guide): it is written in the Sanscrit language, and is explained by twenty-four Purans, or commentaries, and is generally denominated the *Jeyne Shaster;* its author is affirmed to be Vayshava Sayana, a Reshi, or holy person, who, by long and continued prayer and adoration, had acquired a knowledge of divine things. The gods of the Arhitæ, or Jeynes, are the spirits of men rendered perfect, and are termed *Purrim Hauns,* who, owing to their great virtues, have become exempt from change and misfortune, and are all equal

* Researches of the Bombay Literary Society.

in rank and power; they are addressed by various titles, but all tending to one and the same end, such as *Jeyne Ishura*, the Lord Jeyne, arhita (worthy), and sidha (holy): and these names, titles, and attributes are multiplied ad infinitum.

The Sidha, or Purrim Hauns, reside in heaven enjoying Mocsha, or Supreme bliss, or immortality *; and it is the universal opinion of the Jeynes, that through the worship and adoration paid to these Sidhas future happiness can alone be obtained.

The first person among the Jeynes, who, by his virtue,

* The state of bliss by absorption in the Supreme Being, obtained by the aspiring votaries of Jeyne and Bood'h, in becoming Nirvaneh, or beatified, is thus beautifully described by our illustrious countryman, the immortal JONES, in his Hymn to Narayena, or Spirit of God moving on the waters.

——"Hence vanish from my sight!
Delusive pictures, unsubstantial shows!
My soul, absorb'd, one only Being knows,
Of all perceptions one abundant source,
Whence every object, every moment flows;
Suns hence derive their force,
Hence planets learn their course:
But suns, and fading worlds, I view no more;
God only I perceive, God only I adore."

arrived at this elevated station was *Adiparam Ishura*, the first great Sidha; and by worshipping him the favour of all the inferior Sidhas may be obtained. In this farrago of deities we may, without much difficulty, trace the origin of the Jupiter of the Greek and Roman mythology, attended by his cortege of inferior deities. Inferior in rank to the Sidhas are the *Dewtahs*, or deified mortals, whose good works, during their residence on earth, have procured them an inferior heaven, termed *Swerga*, or Paradise, where they are said to enjoy great power and happiness. This heaven is situated in the regions of the air, higher than even Mount Meru, which is the north pole of the Hindoos; and to the inhabitants of this elevated region men are commanded to perform worship, as they possess the power of adding an increase of happiness to their temporal felicity.

Vishnu, from whom the Jeyne deities emanate, was at one time a Rajah, or sovereign prince, who, having performed good works on earth, was again regenerated in the person of Rama, or Rama-Parasa. During the early part of his life he was a great hero, victorious over his enemies. But he afterwards retired from the allurements and pleasures of the world, and became a *Sunniasi*, or recluse, and lived so pure a life that he ultimately attained Sidha, under the name of *Jina*, or complete absolution from sin. In the opinion of the Jeynes, *Maheshura*, or Siva, and Brahma, are acknowledged as Dewtahs, but are inferior in virtue and power to *Indra*, the god of the firmament, who is the chief of all the select beings who inhabit Swerga or Paradise.

In the heaven of Indra are sixteen stages or mansions, containing as many different degrees of Dewtahs, who live in a degree of bliss respectively, agreeably to their merits. An inferior class reside on Mount Meru; but the power and happiness possessed by these are inferior to those of the inhabitants of Swerga, according to the opinions of the Jeynes. Below Mount Meru and the earth is *Bhavana*, or hell, the abode of wicked spirits. These are called Rucshas, and Asoors, evil genii; and although endowed with great power, they are, from their innate wickedness of disposition, for ever miserable. Bhavana, or the hell of the Jeynes, is divided into ten different places of punishment, which are severe in proportion to the crimes committed whilst on earth by their respective inhabitants. Their doctrines of heaven and earth are whimsical. They suppose them never to have been created, but are eternal; but that of the particular portion of the earth called Bharata, or Arya, one-sixth part is liable both to destruction and reproduction. The former is accomplished by a poisonous wind that destroys every thing living; after which a shower of fire consumes the whole of this portion of the universe,—when it is again renovated and revivified by a grateful shower of ghee, or clarified butter *, followed by a second of pure milk, and finally by one of the juice of the sugar-cane. Men and animals then repairing from the other five portions of the earth which are imperishable, inhabit the new Bharata; and things go on in their usual rotation. The books of the *Arhita Loag*, or Jeynes, make mention of Dwypas, or islands, surrounding Mount Meru, of which the one that he inhabits is termed Jambu Dwypa. From hence, according to Jeyne tradition, you proceed as far as *Manushutra*, a mountain situated

* Buchanan, passim.

in Pushcara Dwypa, between which and Jambu Dwypa are two seas and an island termed Dutyah Chandra. Jambu Dwypa is divided into six portions, the inhabitants of five of which are termed *Melechas*, or Baubariases; and Arlirjas, or Bharatis, the portion of the Jeynes, is divided into fifty-six Desas, or countries, two of which are especially assigned to Arabia and China. Every animal, from Indra down to the meanest insect, or the most wicked Racshah, or evil spirit, according to the Jeyne belief, existed from all eternity, i. e. according to the nature of its actions, during its different existences upon earth, will continue * to undergo changes from a higher to a lower rank, or vice versâ, until at length it becomes perfect, and is absorbed in the divinity; but the Sidha, or perfect spirit, before he attains that envied state, must be born once, out of the highest castes; though, in order to become a Brahmin, it is not necessary that he should be born again of a cow—an indispensable qualification amongst the modern Hindoos, or followers of *Vyasa*. The Arhita, or Jeynes, however, admit, that to kill

* Buchanan, passim.

G. Scharf lithog. Printed by C. Hullmandel.

PARUS NAUTH.

from a Sculpture in the Collection of General Stuart.

a cow is equally criminal and sinful as the murder of a man, a woman, or child; but the death of any other animal is not an offence of so heinous a nature. The Jeynes never offer sacrifices of animals, but worship their Dewtahs by prayer, and by the offering of fruits, flowers, and incense, as we have already seen, in a manner similar to the worship performed at the temple of Parus Nauth Ishwara. At Puran Puttun, the ancient capital of Guzerat, Parus Nauth Gowricha is worshipped by his followers, the *Sirawuk Loag*, or Jeynes. This worship, according to tradition, has subsisted for more than three thousand years, and is in universal respect throughout those parts of the peninsula of India where the Jeyne faith obtains, though the modern Brahmins still maintain their ascendancy in spiritual matters. The image of Parus Nauth, which is the object of worship, is of white marble, about a cubit in height, in a sitting posture, and cross-legged, like all the other figures of that deified saint, and has a precious stone fixed between the eyebrows. The ceremonies observed in this worship, according to the Jeyne commentary, termed *Sirawuk Poostuck*, consist of simple adoration, with offerings of money, jewels, and clothes, which become the property of the ministering priests of the idol, who are generally Rajpoots. Votaries of the Jeyne religion crowd to this spot from all parts of India. At the present day the place where worship is performed is in the deserts of Parkur, betwixt Sind and Guzerat *.

* The town of Wadwan, belonging to the Peishwa, on the boundaries of the province of Cutch, has amongst its inhabitants numerous Jeynes. They have a temple here with a hundred figures, represented in white marble; these images of holy men are exactly of the same form, and all seated in the same posture, but they are of different sizes. The dark recess (says the intelligent author of Fifteen Years in India) in which this grand pantheon is displayed, being profusely illuminated, the images having bright sparkling eyes, produce such an effect on the observer at the distance where he is kept, that really the scene is awfully grand.—[See Fifteen Years in India, by an Officer in His Majesty's Service, page 343. London, Longman and Co.]

Thus far the author of Fifteen Years in India, to which it may be added, that the Jeyne sect are known to abound in Guzerat, in Kattywar, and in Cutch, as well as along the banks of the Sind, or Indus; and are undoubtedly the descendants of those Cuthites, who, so many ages back, migrated to the banks of the Indus, as detailed by the learned Bryant [See Bryant's Analysis], and already noticed by the author of this work.

The accomplished orientalist and gallant soldier, my friend Sir John Malcolm, has given a particular instance of overweening insolence of the modern Brahmins over the peaceable and inoffensive Jeynes, in the city of Oujein, the capital of Dowlut Row Sindia, in the Malwah province:

By the orthodox Brahmins, who follow the doctrines of Vyasa, the Jeynes are frequently confounded with the San-

"Six years ago (says Sir John), the Jeynes built a handsome temple at Oujein. A jettee or priest of high character arrived from Guzerat to consecrate it, and to place within the shrine the image of their favourite deity, Parus Nauth; but, on the morning of the day fixed for this purpose, after the ceremony had commenced, and the Jeynes had filled the temple, expecting the arrival of their idol, a Brahmin appeared, conveying an oval stone, from the river Seeprah, which he proclaimed as the emblem of Maha Deo; he was joined by a concourse of other Brahmins and Gosseins, who, arming themselves with bludgeons and stones, soon drove the unarmed Sahokars and Bunneahs from the temple. The rude symbol of Maha Deo was placed in the niche prepared for the Jeyne god, amid the shouts of Brahmins and other Hindoos, and was proclaimed as the overthrower of Jeynes, the all-powerful Maha Deo. The Sahokars and Bunneahs appealed to the governor of the city; but the other tribes were too powerful, and dared his interference in a point of this nature. The authority of Dowlut Row Scindia, to whom reference was made, was treated with no greater respect, and the fear of seeing Oujein deserted, with the prospects of distress at his city and Gwalior (for in both the Jeynes stopped all business, and shut their shops), led that prince to use every means to obtain redress for the violent outrage and insult they had suffered; but his threats and applications were alike derided, and fearing to proceed to extremities in a case of religion, he was obliged to remain satisfied with making what amends he could, by remunerating, in part, the expense which the Jeynes had incurred, and the latter, alike powerless from their comparative smallness of numbers and peaceable habits, were obliged to content themselves with this imperfect regata, or worshippers of Bood'h. Their doctrine has, in many points, a great resemblance to that which is taught in Ava, by the followers of Bood'h. The Jeyne Brahmins abstain from lay affairs, and dress like those who follow the doctrines of Vyasa. Their Gooroos, or chief priests, have the power of fining their followers who cheat, or lie; commit murder, or adultery. The fines are given to the gods; that is to say, to the priest.

The Jeynes extend throughout India, but at present they are not numerous, except in South Canara. They have two sorts of temples, one covered with a roof, and called Busty, and the other an open area, surrounded by a wall, and called Butta, which signifies a hill. In the temples called Butta, the only image of a saint is that of a person named *Gomuta Raya*, who, while on earth, was a powerful king.

It appears manifest that what is in our days termed the Jeyne sect was formerly the only religion known to the inha-

paration, and to bear the additional mortification of seeing the temple they had erected become, chiefly from the manner in which it had been won, the most popular place of worship in all Oujein."—See Malcolm's Account of Central India.

bitants of India; and, generally speaking, it continued unaltered till the period of the Moslem invasion; at which time the present heterogeneous Brahminical system arose upon its ruins, and gradually continued to augment until the reign of *Aurungzeeb*, who, equally hostile to both religions, commenced a bloody persecution and massacres amongst them, overthrew their temples, and in the end almost annihilated every trace of the Jeyne faith, that had for ages prevailed in Hindoostan *.

The modern Brahmins at present obtain religious sway throughout India; and in consequence of reiterated persecutions of the Jeynes within the last thousand years, a host of novel deities have been ingrafted and incorporated upon the

* In a Jeyne Purana we find, that when Vishnu was manifested in the *Bood'h outar*, at that period the religion of Jeyne obtained throughout the greater part of Hindoostan. This occurred in the *Tirta Yog*, or second age of mankind; at which period, likewise, three principal personages appeared, Parus Nauth, Bheem Nauth, and Bagheir Nauth, who formed the twenty-fourth *outar*, or incarnation of the Supreme Being in his three representatives: and hence arose the worship of Jeyne and Bood'h.

ancient stock; or rather, we may affirm, the ancient objects of superstition are disguised by new appellations.

The whole of the foregoing documents being taken into due consideration, it is evident that, after a long and bloody struggle between the modern Brahmins and Boodhists, the latter being completely overthrown, the Samana Boodhists then migrated to Thibet, to the country of the Mogul Tartars, to China and Japan; where, as before seen, they fixed their religion and laws. But a very singular remark has been made by the learned Baron Humboldt *, in his elaborate Researches in New Spain, on the great continent of America, wherein he mentions his intention of examining not only the Mexican traditions respecting the destruction of the world by the deluge, but also to prove that traces of the *Trimorti*, or Indian trinity, are absolutely to be found in the religion of the Peruvians; a most remarkable circumstance, and strongly tending to corroborate an idea which I have all along entertained, namely, that the whole system of Pagan idolatry

* Humboldt's Researches in New Spain, translated by Miss Williams.

throughout the world carries with it a strong and striking affinity, collectively and separately; and that, with the single exception of the ordinations of Moses, and the establishment of the Jewish religion, its rites and ceremonies, by the divine dispensation, the system appears in its general bearings to be one and the same thing; until the glorious sun of Christianity, bursting forth with a splendour wholly irresistible, dispelled the clouds of darkness and superstition which had so long overshadowed the Pagan world, and finally brought to light the Gospel of our blessed Saviour, and the establishment of the Christian religion. Since that period, and after a revolution of eighteen centuries, we perceive the most happy results obtaining in various parts of the habitable globe, and have reason for supposing its final triumph will, under the auspices and protection of the great Creator of the universe, and in his own good time, be rendered complete.

APPENDIX.

I.

AURUNGZEBE.

The Bood'h figure lately presented by me to the Royal Asiatic Society of Great Britain and Ireland was procured during a journey made to the district of Jungle Terry in 1819, for the purpose of elucidating the site of ancient Palibothra. It was dug out of the earth, from the side of a large tank, near the ruins of the city of Jeynaggur, where it had been deposited by the natives, most probably at the time of the persecution above mentioned, in order to save it from destruction; as was also another figure of Kanyah, the Apollo of the Hindoos, presented to my friend, Henry Philip Hope, Esquire, of New Norfolk Street. The latter figure had lain so long in the earth that young shoots of trees had taken root within the cavities of the figure, and were obliged to be removed previous to putting it up in my veranda at Bhaugulpore. They were both several feet under ground. —Author.

II.

In a letter received from my friend Mordaunt Ricketts, Esquire, the British Resident at the court of Oude, he there details some particulars of the Jeynes, which I am tempted to offer to the public in a supplementary note. These remarks are dated from Seringapatam, the capital of Mysore, which my friend visited in 1805.

"There are still extant," says Mr. Ricketts, "some historical poems of the Jeynes, relating their destruction by the Brahmins, in several dialects of the Peninsula, such as the *Chintamani*, which is written in poetical Tamul, and there are traditions concerning them in almost every part of the country. The persecution in which they were ruined was chiefly fomented by *Sankara Acharya*, a great leader of one of the Hindoo sects. One tradition at Seringapatam is, that during the reign of a certain rajah of Mysore, while the Brahmins and Jeynes existed conjointly, a considerable controversy occurred concerning the moon's age, between the reciters of the *Panganyam* belonging to the Jeynes and Brahminical sects. At last the rajah, being enraged, swore to destroy without mercy the sect which should be found to be erroneous in their calculations.

"The Jeyne calculations, from their superior skill in astronomy, were really correct, and those of the Brahmins erroneous; but the latter, in their exigency, had recourse to one of their holy men, at a signal by whom, the moon, contrary to the laws of nature, suddenly appeared in heaven, to verify the Brahminical imposture. On this the most merciless persecution was instantly fomented by the Jeynes. It is curious that the Brahmins should preserve this relation.

"The Jeynes claim to themselves the composition of the Vedas, and the original materials of the Pooranas, and, indeed, of the principal books possessed by the Brahmins. From the whole train of their tenets, it is impossible to consider them as any other than a Brahminical sect, though differing from the common belief in many essential particulars. According to some, Bood'h is the sect of Jeynes; but the Jeynes of Mysore disdain any connexion with the Boodhists, and when they rise in the morning, the first thing they do is to recite a curse or imprecation on the Brahmins.

"The Jeynes are a religious sect which differs in many respects from the Brahmins, especially in the worship of fire. They reckon their own to have been the primitive religion.

"The Jeynes should abstain from the following things:

"From eating at night; slaying any animals; eating the fruit of those trees which yield milk, pumpkins, young bamboo plants; from eating honey; from flesh; from taking away the wealth of others; taking by violence a married woman; eating flowers, butter, or cheese; and worshipping the gods of another religion. To abandon these entirely is to be a proper Jeyne. They never drink intoxicating liquors. They never observe funeral ceremonies, for their law says: The spirit is separate or distinct from the body, which is composed of five elementary parts, that return to their former states after burning; to the deceased, therefore, no ceremony is due.

"A man of superior abilities and knowledge should feed himself with *Ghee*, or clarified butter, the best food while he lives in the world; for his body never returns after it is burnt.

"What a man giveth, eateth, or drinketh in this world is of no advantage to him, for he carries nothing with him at his end.

"A man of sense should believe only what he sees with his own eyes, and should never believe what he hears from others. The foolish people of other tribes, being deficient in knowledge, spend money in vain, on account of their deceased relations; for how can a dead man feel any satisfaction in the performing of ceremonies, and the feeding of others? A lamp no longer gives light by having oil enter it, after the flame is extinguished.

"To abstain from slaughter is perfection, to kill any living creature is a sin.

"For the information of mankind be it known, that the foundation of ages, or times, is countless. We ought, therefore, to believe that humankind are ignorant of the true knowledge of the origin of things, which is known only to the Almighty; whose state is without beginning, and end, who has obtained eternal victory over the frailty of nature and earthly affections. The Jeynes, nevertheless, do not believe in a God dwelling in the Heavens, because none has seen him; but they worship their high priests, who, by sublime penance, have risen above the frailties of human nature, as images, or incarnations of the invisible God; of whom they say, that he has no likeness, and that his body may be compared to an image of transparent crystal.

"The Jeynes reckon two great periods of time, which they term *Voocharpereea* and *Avasarpereea*, which revolve constantly, and each of which contains six inferior divisions. The first period, *Avasarpereea*; the second great division is termed *Shoocama*, contains likewise four inferior divisions, or ages, during which the fertility of the earth, and human stature, and human virtues gradually decreased till the beginning of the fourth age, when mankind were reduced to miserable savages. At this period Prooshbanund *Teartaroo* was incarnated, to teach the knowledge of good and evil; and, if possible, to arrange the duties and occupations of men, and to instruct them to acquire the advantages of earth and heaven.

"He divided mankind into four great classes, Brahmins, Chutrees, Veasyas, and Soodras, after whom came the Pariars. He composed many books in the Sanscrit language, amongst which is the *Amra Lingham*.

" The original languages, which the Jeynes used, were the Sanscrit and Pracrit; but the greater part of their ancient books are, at present, written in the ancient Canara character.

" Their modern Pagodas were founded by *Chanover Daroy*, the prime minister of Rajah Muttu Jeyne, king of Madura. In their chronologies they say, that after the reigns of the Jeyne sovereigns, there reigned the Chotturoos, or Rajahs, of the Chuttree caste, the Ballaroos, or Ballies, until the reign of Begul Rajah, when the Dekhan was conquered by the modern Brahmins. The Dekhan, after this, remained under the authority of the Rajah of Bijanugur, or *Worongola*, until the Mahomedans, in their turn, attacked and conquered it."

THE END.

DIRECTIONS FOR PLACING THE PLATES.